Your
management
sucks

ALSO BY MARK STEVENS

Your Marketing Sucks

Your management sucks

WHY YOU
HAVE TO DECLARE
WAR ON YOURSELF...
AND YOUR
BUSINESS

Mark Stevens

CROWN
BUSINESS
NEW YORK

Copyright © 2006 by Mark Stevens

All rights reserved.
Published in the United States by Crown Business, an imprint of the
Crown Publishing Group, a division of Random House, Inc., New York.
www.crownpublishing.com

Crown Business is a trademark and the Rising Sun colophon is a
registered trademark of Random House, Inc.

Library of Congress Cataloging-in-Publication Data
Stevens, Mark, 1947–
    Your management sucks : why you have to declare war on
yourself . . . and your business / Mark Stevens.
        1. Management   I. Title.
    HD31.S6926   2006
    658.4–dc22   2005031679

ISBN-13: 978-1-4000-5493-0
ISBN-10: 1-4000-5493-1

Printed in the United States of America

DESIGN BY BARBARA STURMAN

10 9 8 7 6 5 4 3 2 1

First Edition

We all have two choices:

TO ACCEPT WHO AND WHERE WE ARE IN LIFE

or

TO STRIVE FOR WHAT WE CAN BECOME
AND WHERE THAT CAN TAKE US.

— MARK STEVENS

Contents

Your
management
sucks

Introduction

A Work in Progress:
Why You Must Take
a Hike from the
Land of Business
as Usual

Before You Tell Me to Get Lost

In the time it took you to pick up this book and glance at the cover, chances are you started thinking:

Is Stevens crazy? *Where does he get the gall to tell me that my management sucks? He doesn't even know me, or how I rate as a manager. Furthermore, he wants me to declare war on myself. What's this all about?*

It's about something simple and profound. And if you hang in there with me, you will see that it is about something critical to the success of your career. Allow me to put this in a personal context for a moment.

No one has to tell me to "take a hike." I tell it to myself all the time. Not as a rebuke, but as a reward. As a reminder that what often appears to be the center of action in business—and in one's personal life—is really a sideshow. A distraction. It is vitally important to keep moving back to where the real action lies.

What do I mean by this and what does it have to do with taking a hike? My business—called MSCO—was founded on an idea. Over time, the idea evolved, grew in size and scope, and was fused with new ideas. As I took this ever-broader offering to market, my company grew in tandem. Not that this corporate growth was neatly aligned and perfectly synchronized with the intellectual firepower driving it. Far from it. There were plenty of fits and starts, static periods, and times when the ideas were bigger and better than the business. And vice versa. Instinctively, I understood that this imbalance is part of the process of building a business and that just as my love as a parent sometimes eclipsed my skills as a dad, if I kept striving to perfect the model of Mark Stevens and his business, ultimately the elements would converge, producing the progress I was seeking.

I must tell you that there were times when everything did appear to be aligned. When the ideas and the business were in harmony. Because neither had to catch up with the other, my world seemed to be orderly. Peaceful. I could take it easy. Life was good.

Well, yes and no. Fortunately my antennae warned me that what felt like solace was really a prelude to complacency. No business has ever grown over time by allowing ideas and execution to remain in harmony. Neither has any manager ever grown over the years by seeking and indulging in tranquillity. Nice fairy tale, but it fails to produce the fission from which breakthroughs emerge.

Think of our nation's founding fathers: Jefferson, Franklin, Adams. These guiding lights were always generating more ideas than they could possible bring to fruition. But they kept rolling forward, thinking and dreaming and inventing; and even though only a fraction of their ideas turned into tangible products, they brought us great universities, daring expeditions, breakthrough experiments, enlightened declarations, an extraordinary constitution, and the world's longest-enduring republic.

In my own, far-humbler way, I recognized that I needed to continuously develop new ideas that would force my business into a constant state of catch-up. In the process, I experienced the epiphany that the day-to-day slugfest in the office—meetings with employees, seeing customers, engaging in conference calls, catching the red-eye to L.A.—is

The Land of Business as Usual. The place where you are too busy executing to innovate. I knew I had to get out. To take a hike. A thousand hikes.

So I ventured off to Ward Pound Ridge Reservation, a wilderness preserve about five miles from my home. Hardly ever a soul there. Just me and my dog and a pad (which has now morphed into a BlackBerry). I walk and think. I sit under an oak tree and think. In summer, I put my feet in a stream and think. The only rules are that I don't think about anything tactical. I think about new ideas. New components of my philosophy. Perhaps a whole new philosophy. Everything is open to examination. To rethinking. For more than a decade, this is where I have turned to reinvent myself. To grow. To develop the ideation for an ever-better business. An ever-richer life. Some years ago I heard the wonderful story of how Edwin Land was struck with the brainstorm for inventing instant photography. Walking down a street in Cambridge, Massachusetts, Dr. Land suddenly saw his daughter's wide eyes looking up at him: "Dad, how come we can't see a photo as soon as we take one?"

Just as he was about to espouse conventional wisdom as to why that would be impossible, Land checked himself and instead wondered, "Why not, indeed?"

Until that unexpected turning point in his life, Land thought of the laboratory as the center of the action. But on that magical day he recognized that the laboratory didn't hold a candle to a stroll in the sun with his daughter. It was Land's hike. Do you have one? A way to extricate yourself from the bouillabaisse of daily to-dos to engage in the power of ideas. Whatever form your "hike" takes, it can drive your strategy as you manage your business unit and your life. Without it, you may be very busy, but doing what? And going where? This book will help you ask these questions and find the answers.

As you move through life, nurturing a career, or building a business, you face the option of doing what comes naturally or—and this is a BIG or—driving yourself to achieve a higher standard. Pursuing relentless improvement. Continuously assessing every aspect of what you do and how you do it with the determination to raise the bar.

This means declaring war on yourself. Constructive war, to be sure, but war nevertheless. Passive people who are willing to accept themselves for what they are without the drive and the will and the passion and the pedal-to-the-metal conviction to improve themselves may appear to have a certain kind of personal solace, but they will always be left in the dust by those who seek bigger, better, richer rewards by rejecting what is and aspiring to what can be.

This is especially true for anyone who manages (or has the ambition to do so) anything. A company. A department. A business unit. Whether you are first starting out in business or are a seasoned pro, the need to declare constructive war on yourself is ever present. It means that you will never accept things the way they are. Instead, you will drive yourself to learn more, think more creatively, pursue innovation, and demand excellence in everything you do and/or are involved with.

Extraordinary managers aren't extraordinary by dint of their DNA alone. In the course of my career, I've had the privilege of meeting and working with scores of them. All are dramatically different men and women drawn from disparate backgrounds and operating in widely diverse industries, but united by a nonstop determination to keep upping the ante on themselves and (through osmosis and directive) on those reporting to them.

There is a powerful dynamic at work here. Anyone who achieves success as a manager, as a businessperson, as a leader, views his life as a work in progress. Rather than accepting who or what you are as the finished product frozen in place by genetics or fate, you keep driving to a higher level of knowledge, experience, talent, and, ultimately, performance. In effect, you are determined to leave your former self behind as the model of what can be inspires your personal growth.

We all respect the young athlete who practices day and night to achieve the highest levels of professional accomplishment. Jimmy Connors standing on a court practicing his serve until it is too dark to see. Tiger Woods practicing his putt until he lands in the pantheon of golf's greatness and then puts his determination into overdrive, pursuing the next Tiger and the next Tiger and the next Tiger that he believes resides within the unlimited potential of himself. The passive among us advise that we should be "comfortable within our own skin," but the truly successful reject this, shedding their skin as they march toward the new and continuously more effective embodiment of themselves. All of their lives they declare constructive war, knowing that this is the route to extraordinary performance and the spoils of success that go with it.

Some years ago, I spent time alone with Bill Gates on the Microsoft campus. Of all the impressions that have stayed with me from that day, none is more indelible than Gates's lifelong commitment to declare war on himself.

BILL GATES: I toss and turn at night thinking about the kid in a garage who is gunning for Microsoft . . . for me. There's never a day that I feel safe, impervious to competitors. The only way this company can prevail is if it keeps getting smarter and smarter. Exponentially smarter.

As the Microsoft CEO, the same principle applies to me.

When people ask me if I think I'm smart, my answer is "not smart enough." The world keeps moving forward, and I have to stay ahead of the curve. The way I view it, there's not a minute to waste. You know that dead time we experience when we get out of our cars and walk into our homes. I've decided to turn that into productive time. So I mount educational material on the garage wall. Right now, I have a map of Africa up there. Instead of staring into space as I move from car door to front door, I glance at the map. Day by day, a part of the world I don't know enough about sinks in, and when I feel I know the geography of Africa well, something else will get tacked to that wall.

Great leaders never stop learning. Never stop driving themselves to be better today than they were yesterday. To know more. To uncover mysteries. To fill gaps. It's their way of declaring constructive war on themselves. They know that once they get complacent, someone lurking around the corner will eat their lunch.

For years, former Citigroup CEO Sandy Weill kept a sign in his office:

THE BOSS ISN'T HAPPY

This was Sandy's in-your-face way of saying, "As long as I'm running this place, we're declaring war on the business every day."

I remember when my wife and I vacationed at the Cap Juluca resort on the island of Anguilla. The resort owner, Dion Friedland, happened to be at his resort at the time. A gregarious South African, he regaled us with stories of his years in Johannesburg, where he earned his fortune building Dion stores into the largest chain of discount stores in South Africa.

At the time—when Friedland's business was generating $200 million in annual sales and Wal-Mart was in the multibillions—Dion received a letter from Sam Walton, asking if he could visit him to learn his *secrets of success*.

Astounding! Here was the Global King of Discount retailing seeking to *learn* from a guy who built a business a fraction of the size of Wal-Mart. But to Walton he was simply following one of the fundamental rules for wise and enlightened management: Anytime you can learn from anyone, anywhere, seize the opportunity. To Sam, every day was the right time to declare constructive war on himself. To be a smarter, wiser, broader-thinking Sam Walton than he was the day before.

Dion Friedland remembers the visit with twenty-twenty vision.

Walton arrived in Johannesburg with a pad and tape recorder and spent every waking moment talking to and interviewing my employees, my customers, and me. He was the greatest retailer who ever lived and he was on a mission to learn, to better himself, to prep for success as if he was a kid in college preparing for his first job at Woolworth's. If there was a way to wake up each day as a new and improved Sam Walton, he was going to find it. I always called Sam Walton the best brain-picker who ever lived. Sam wasn't the best innovator and he certainly wasn't the most creative retailer I've ever met. But he had a unique ability to gather your best ideas, to take them back to his company, and then to implement and execute them better than anyone else.

I'm so passionate about the need, the benefit, and the power of declaring constructive war that I did it to myself, to my company, my employees, and my clients. I'll tell you the full story later on, but whoa, what I did was more than a garden-variety corporate reorganization. It was a personal and commercial upheaval—a painful, challenging, and exhilarating event that altered my life. An event I could easily have avoided. An event I chose to endure because I viewed myself and my company as a work in progress, and I had to act decisively and dramatically to achieve my goal. Painful? Yes. Difficult? Yes. Complex? Yes. High risk? Yes. But success demands that you face up to all of this, bite the bullet, and move ahead, knowing the real thing is never easy or certain or risk free. I'm thankful every day that I took the risk and accepted the challenge. And that I continue to do so.

This isn't idle talk. It is at the core of the risk-and-reward equation that drives greatness. Everyone talks about growing a business or managing a business unit. Nurturing it. Guiding it. The care and feeding of it. And on and on and on . . . ad nauseam. Chalk it all up to so much B-school blather. Ninety-nine percent of the time it's just words. Feelgood messages that lead to high fives and corporate cheers and blah, blah, blah . . . but no new growth.

Why is this holding pattern so common? So frustrating? So costly and unproductive? Because there are two overriding obstacles in the way of growing your business/business unit/department. And they can obstruct your straight-line path to managerial excellence:

1. You have no compelling strategy for growth, nor does anyone else in the company (don't point to your mission statement, that's just wallpaper).

Note that I said compelling strategy. You may work hard and wish hard and even have a plan laid out in a colorful PowerPoint presentation, but chances are it doesn't identify with power and precision how you will exploit opportunities, combat challenges, and grow profitability.

It's a document, and documents don't drive growth.

2. **Y**our people like to stay squarely in their comfort thrones.

Yes, *thrones.* Because you lack a compelling and dynamic strategy for growth, the people who work for you (be it one or a hundred thousand) may lack direction. In this environment, they become overly focused on protecting what they have (position, power, authority, place in the hierarchy) as opposed to seeking new opportunities and demonstrating that they can excel at them.

It's a throne because the manager who fails to create a sense of urgency, of opportunity, of continuous growth and progress, often creates a sense of entitlement among employees.

It is their job because *it is their job*—solid performance, they believe, is another matter.

In the most egregious cases, employees come to believe

they are paid through *divine intervention*. Growth or not, the paychecks will keep coming (hey, capitalism is really a privately owned entitlement program, isn't it?).

If you have been managing for any amount of time, you have experienced the symptoms of this malaise. So often I hear managers moan, "I can't get these people to do what I want them to do. They have their own agenda, damn it." Hold on a moment. "These people" may be the IT department or the sales folks or a renegade group in human resources, but whoever they are, they cannot have their own agenda. Not unless a weak manager allows them to. Every chain of command has a boss, and that person must set the agendas. Simple, right? In theory, yes, but not in practice. That's why so many companies have bands of "outlaws" doing what they damn well feel like doing even if it goes against management's directives.

In a classic case, the CEO of an Israeli-based biotech firm complained to me that he was having trouble engineering a turnaround (the company had gone into bankruptcy before he was called in to right the ship) because he couldn't get the sales and marketing people to focus on the major pharmaceutical companies, where the big opportunities lay.

MS: Where do they focus?

CEO: On small labs, and small labs place small orders, and we can't get a foot off the ground with small orders.

MS: Have you advised them that they are approaching the wrong targets?

CEO: Of course.

MS: And?

CEO: And they keep on courting the small labs.

MS: Why would they do that?

CEO: Because that's where they are comfortable. Our sales and marketing people are scientists and the guys at the labs are also scientists, and they like to talk to their peers. The idea of visiting a big pharma company scares the hell out of them.

MS: Have you thought of replacing them?

CEO: I've thought of it.

MS: And?

CEO: Well, it's not so easy. Their coworkers like them. And finding good salespeople is always a challenge. And, well, yes, I should replace them, but . . .

Sorry, but in scenarios like this, there are no "buts." When the people who have to sell aren't selling and the others who have to produce aren't producing and on and on, THERE'S NO COMPANY. TURN AROUND, CLOSE YOUR EYES, AND IN A NANOSECOND, THE BUSINESS VANISHES.

How does this happen? In many cases, it's because you as the manager/CEO/owner have become comfortable or, worse yet, complacent (ready to admit that?).

This stuff gets surreal—more often than people want to admit. One of my client companies built a fabulous business providing Cold War consulting advice to corporate clients doing business with the Pentagon and U.S. defense companies. For decades, the company's growth trajectory knew only one direction: due north.

And then the world began to morph, but the company refused to change with it. Why should it? Management was rich. Employees were well paid. Perks dotted the landscape like Caribbean palm trees. But in this land of plenty, this picture-perfect postcard, things turned ugly. Slowly at first, and then with increasing velocity.

The reason: the Berlin Wall fell, the Cold War became a thing of the past, and the demand for the company's services dried up. Contracts with the Fortune 100 (the core of the company's business) declined to the point that the business nose-dived into the red and projections showed no relief in sight.

Shocked by the projections (only because no one had been asking tough questions about the company's shrinking contract base for years), management called an emergency meeting. Here another problem surfaced: Few of the attendees thought there was an emergency. Hardly anyone saw reason for alarm. Why? Because management failed to set a clear course for growth, because it became complacent, and because it allowed employees to live in a suspended state of animation disconnected from the realities of the marketplace, no one took the threat seriously. They grew so used to Moscow/Washington tensions, they believed they would always bring the world to the brink . . . and, in any case, the company would simply thrive because it always had.

There is nothing evil at work here. No one sets out to create this sorry state. It is simply a reflection of human behavior (which, as a manager, you must guard against).

 think of it as the shooting-fish-in-a-barrel syndrome.

When a business grows beyond initial projections, once it appears to defy gravity and build a powerful momentum, managers can become intoxicated by this magic-carpet ride and believe that from that moment on the future is golden. Guaranteed. A sure thing. And that's when they put the plane on autopilot and a hard landing looms in the not-so-distant future.

Which leads us back to the comfort throne. Sure, you should pursue growth. Every enterprise must consciously move ahead or it inevitably falls behind. And it is your managerial obligation—at every stage in your career—to make certain to move upstream armed with a compelling strategy and a team empowered and motivated to drive it. But there is no sense in playing at it. Giving it lip service. Pretending the world and your marketplace haven't changed. Faking it. Putting on a puppet show. You have to lead it with all of the octane at your disposal. Or admit you're not up to it and accept the consequences.

OK, what are the consequences? Think of it this way:

very business can only move in one of four directions.

Grow slowly

Grow **rapidly**

Go out of business slowly

Go out of business **rapidly**

Let me explain. Most successful companies—those that endure for many years—go through this cycle. It is widely believed that the decline, even for the great companies, is inevitable. When the likes of Woolworth's, A&P, and Zenith careered from the heights, there was no shock. All were viewed as victims of changing times. The Harvard Business School develops case studies on the ebbs and flows in corporate life cycles as if there must be an ebb and flow. But I don't buy that for a second. To me it is merely a symptom of management that loses its bearings or its vision or its drive or its healthy sense of paranoia about tomorrow—and what it will bring. All are behavior symptoms you can and should identify and address in managing your department or company.

Start by recognizing that the art and science of management is made overly complex. That's because conventional wisdom holds that managers must be well versed and up to the minute on 1,001 issues, processes, disciplines, and initiatives. That sounds fine, but it happens to be impossible.

Instead of viewing your business unit as dozens or hundreds or thousands of anything, focus on a few key elements or indicators, and your performance can soar. I love the way Jack Welch encapsulated this into his managerial approach and leadership expectations when he was running GE. All of the sprawling company's business units had to be number one or two in their industry or they would be sold. Jack could have written chapter and verse about the managerial methodologies he expected from his senior team, but instead he made it crystal clear and powerfully simple. Any manager who failed to meet the one-two test lost his business unit. And his halo. And his chance to soar up the GE chain of command. Why get convoluted in your messaging when something so straightforward can drive smart and talented people to stay up all night figuring out how to succeed. Current GE CEO Jeff Immelt now carries on the legacy, holding his lieutenants to the same industry-leadership acid test. What better way to motivate them and judge their performance. (My company has served GE business units, and we know from the inside out what that pressure feels like. When our client Storage USA (SUSA) failed to jump into the one-two winners' circle, Jeff sold them to Prudential.)

Simplify the issues, and you will see your realities and your options for dealing with them with greater clarity.

Let's focus on *going out of business.* Just when they are euphoric over their initial success, the managers of growing companies (as illustrated by the Cold-War consulting business) get complacent ("Hey, this juggernaut can't be stopped"). Blinded by the giddy euphoria of the moment, they take their hands off the helm and start to slowly but inexorably decline. Because the first signs of trouble are modest dips in sales and/or profits that barely register on the Richter scale, it hardly looks at first like a *going-out-of-business-slowly* scenario. Just a temporary blip or a harmless hiccup. Everyone blames the decline on the economy or some other factors beyond their control, no one changes, and then bam—the company plummets down a slippery slope as an off year turns into a problem. And a problem into a precipitous decline. And a precipitous decline into a free fall . . . and suddenly the going-out-of-business-slowly syndrome accelerates into disasterville.

The bigger the company or business unit, the longer it can postpone the inevitable (because it can marshal a greater financial cushion to camouflage and delay the doomsday scenario it is careening toward). But this only disguises the fact that the company is spiraling downward, the victim of its own:

COMPLACENCY

DECEPTION

FEAR OF A BAD DAY

FAILURE TO ACT

hich takes us back to our mission. To prevent this—and to achieve perpetual growth—you have to declare war.

"Why?" you ask again.

Reread the obstacles to growing your business and achieving perpetual growth (on pages 21–22). View them as gremlins. As viruses. Recognize that they do not go away on their own. They dig in. They respond to halfhearted managerial attacks by regrouping themselves and blocking growth.

f you are really serious about growing your business (if you're not, you should get a job with the Postal Service), you have to don your battle jacket and attack these obstacles/roadblocks/gremlins because . . . because every day you play Mr. Rogers, they are attacking you . . . and they are winning!

The warning signs that you must declare constructive war extend far beyond the attitudes and work practices of employees to include a wide scope of issues impacting the way your enterprise creates, delivers, and services its products.

Think of them as Code Red signs.

All are reason to declare war. Let's explore a few now.

- Your customers LIKE your products and/or services. The problem is, LIKE isn't good enough. People buy when they FALL IN LOVE, not when they FALL IN LIKE. Time to raise the bar.

hen customers FALL IN LOVE, they:

Buy quickly
Buy often
Buy more than they need
Buy more than they can afford
Remain customers for life

Let's put this through a coffee filter (of sorts). Everywhere you go, people are selling you coffee: in restaurants, roadside diners, gasoline service stations, department stores, food courts, ballparks—the stuff is brewing in millions of pots right now. And most of it ranks from OK to mediocre. So you buy it when it's convenient, and you don't when it's not. And one thing is clear: You're never driven to patronize the purveyors of run-of-the-mill java just to partake of a cup of brown water.

And then there's the coffee 23 million people go out of their way to drink every day. The coffee they adore. The coffee they crave. The coffee they MUST HAVE at almost any price. Starbucks coffee.

Of all the factors that have contributed to the Starbucks juggernaut, none is more important than the fact that the company has created a product that people love. Adore. Yearn for. But most companies stop trying to surpass the "like" mark, and that's why there's only one Starbucks. And one Google. And one Apple. And one Prada.

- You find it hard to get out of bed in the morning. The thought of going to work is less than thrilling. Bad! Bad! Bad! You should be springing out of bed. Something is getting in the way: politics or inefficiency or complacency. You're not sure which it is or how to get to the root of it—and are thus defenseless. Even worse, you are a victim of your own enterprise. As a result, the company fails to grow at a significant rate, in part because the *leader* is like a pilot lost in fog.

- Customers are complaining about *this, that, or the other thing.* Although it's easy to dismiss this with "They are just a bunch of gripes," the fact is that the market speaks the truth. Something is wrong in your shop. Fix it.

- Your team rarely comes up with new ideas. When someone has the temerity to put an idea on the table—particularly one that is innovative or, heaven forbid, even daring—everyone finds reason to stab it to death. To swear it won't work. This may be fine for the United Nations, but it is a guaranteed way to make sure that your company falls victim to the *wild-eyed dreamers* known as the competition. Specifically, those who recognize that every product and service can always be vastly improved—and are determined to do just that. (Think of them as two guys in a garage. And be assured they have you in their crosshairs.)

Waging continuous war on yourself (and in turn on your business unit) is the hallmark of exceptional managers. And it should be yours. Starting today. The failure to do so means the business unit under your watch—the one that impacts the course of your career and your wealth—will deteriorate. That's a promise . . . and, yes, a threat!

The Insight That Will Change Your Life

 hen I say, "Your management sucks," I'm talking to myself as well.

At one time or another, we all fail to perform as well as we can. And once we raise the bar, our world changes, and we have to drive to new heights again. The most important point is to understand and accept this need for continuous improvement.

The good news is that you can dramatically rethink your managerial perspective, approach, and style. All change is incremental, but the approach outlined in this book delivers immediate results that grow in scope and power over time.

 know this to be true because I have waged war on myself and my business.

I have advised thousands of businesspeople, from CEOs to novice managers, helping them to identify challenges and opportunities and gremlins and enemies and allies, and stood side by side with them as we worked together to grow their businesses. That's how this book, this course, came to be. It is fashioned from experience. On the ground. In factories and boardrooms, in retail stores and high-tech centers, in New York and Pittsburgh and Shanghai and Zurich. It is a crash course because it drives right to the source of the issues, attacks them with a vengeance, pays no heed to political correctness, and maintains a constant sense of urgency. This isn't about getting an A on a thesis; it's about powering careers and driving profits. Period.

I have helped many businesspeople who have lost their management compasses to reestablish direction at all stages and levels of their careers. Over the years, my professional role underwent an interesting transformation:

 evolved from being my clients' adviser to becoming their secretary of war.

Their comrade in arms. The guy they turn to when the business is going great guns and they need to impose discipline and controls to keep the growth profitable and maintain the quality of their products and services. The guy they turn to when the business is slipping and they're not sure why. Or when they know why but need a partner they can confide in and then trust to engineer a recovery and go into battle with them.

Most managers—at some point in their rise through the ranks—need the insights, the process, the self-discipline, and the willpower to climb to the next level. To outmaneuver internal competitors. To find a way to distinguish themselves as exceptional. Or to package what is already exceptional and broadcast it to the powers that be.

That's where I come in. That's where this book comes in. It helps to enhance and package your skills, expertise, philosophy, methodology, and personal marketing to establish you as a superb manager. A warrior.

Let's get started.

Unleashing the Power of a Personal Philosophy

One morning in the year 2001, I woke up and thought to myself, "I've built a nice company. There are fifty-seven people in my employ . . . I've got a full client roster . . . MSCO Inc. is profitable.

"Very profitable."

T hen I meandered downstairs to have coffee with my wife and said, "Honey, I'm going to fire everybody."

She said, "What are you talking about?"

(I get that a lot.)

So I explained.

"We've got a team of good people. And good people can build a nice company . . . but they can't build a great one. So I'm going to fire everybody and start recruiting only the really top performers in every business discipline. When we built this business, we viewed it as a work in progress, always tinkering with all gears and levers to make it better. And better. But one day, for who knows what reason, we stopped. Or maybe I should say *I* stopped. But no more."

Looking back, I'm not sure my wife believed I was serious. More like first-thoughts-in-the-morning wishful thinking. But I knew from the moment that I announced my war plan over a bowl of Shredded Wheat, I was armed and dangerous and ready to go.

Not that it was a whim. For a year or so I'd been thinking about it, ruminating over it, assessing the risks, dreaming of the benefits, and exploring the implications. I founded MSCO on the principle that the marketplace was lacking a new kind of entity—a hybrid between a marketing firm and a strategic consultancy—and I pulled it all together and developed a methodology and created a brand and built a team and secured clients and went through the trial and error, the donnybrook, the roller-coaster wonder of making it all work.

The roots of the business trace back to a warm June day right around my twenty-second birthday. As a hard-core, antiestablishment, I'll-do-it-my-way 1960s kid, I had taken a zigzag route to career and the workplace. High school held little interest for me. (Living in the New York City borough of Queens, I could always—any time of year—pick up a girlfriend and drive out to Jones Beach. So who the hell wanted to sit in a dreary cell of a classroom in the dreary prison of a building called Bayside High School? Not Mark Stevens.) Next I meandered through a third-rate college—took off a semester to care for my family upon the death of my father (who left us $84, no hard assets, and Himalayan bills), and later on I took off another semester student-partying on $5 a day in Paris.

Funny story there. I went to Paris with the $300 I inherited when my grandmother died (I lost my dad and my beloved maternal grandparents all in eighteen months). Naturally, I'm living in pathetic dumps, but the wine is cheap and the girls are amazing and I spend my summer days as the only guy lying in the sun on a French houseboat (the *Piscine Deligny*) with two hundred women in Band-Aid bikinis. Life was good, and then it got better.

One of the girls I was dating—the wealthy daughter of an even wealthier Parisian businessman—was moving to Algeria for some crazy social cause and asked me to house-sit her splendiferous pied-à-terre overlooking superposh Place de Victor Hugo. So there I was with a pauper's wallet and I'm bringing dates back from discos to this smasheroo place and they're thinking, "Yeeow, I've got me a rich American."

Anyway, I got sick and wound up in the American Hospital of Paris. Economics dictated that I return home, so I went straight from the *rues de Paris* to the streets of New York once again, finished school, and wound up taking a job at Texaco, working on a magazine they publish to teach their service-station guys (who were much more interested in reading *Jugs* than the rag I was working on) how to sell more tires, batteries, and accessories. Fuuuuuuun!

For the first time in my life, I took a close-up look at the American workplace—Fortune 100 style—and yikes, I didn't like what I saw. My reaction was more like "Get me the hell out of here now!" All of these middle-aged folks are basically sleeping at their desks and then lining up for lunches the size of Thanksgiving Day feasts at 12:00 sharp. After that a nice nap with the office door closed and then out the door at 4:59.

Needless to say, I had plenty of time on my hands at Texaco (I could do a month's worth of assigned tasks in a day), but instead of joining the chorus of deep snoring, I started daydreaming. About possibilities. For new businesses, of all things. And it struck the former sixties idealist (me) that there was a void in the media for a syndicated newspaper column that would provide advice to small-business owners. And to make a long story short, I contacted the Long Island newspaper *Newsday* with the idea and they said yes ("If you show us what you can do by writing twelve columns for free") and I was off and running. In no time, I was self-employed, the head of a fledgling media business that kept growing over the years, increasing revenues and expanding in scope until it evolved into MSCO—a global marketing firm advising senior managers of small, midsize, and very large companies on how to grow their businesses.

And just when the company ascended to a level of success I hadn't dreamed of when I formed the nucleus twenty-five years before during the Texaco days—and there was every reason to heed the axiom "If ain't broken, don't fix it"—I decided to reengineer it from the ground up. To face the fact that MSCO was, is, and always will be a work in progress. I had built a successful business, but I feared that unless I declared war on myself, the enterprise I managed would succumb to mediocrity, and I wasn't going to be part of that. At the time, MSCO was good at identifying precisely why companies were failing to grow at a substantial pace or were poorly managing explosive growth in a way that would enable them to build on their success. We had insight and know-how and an uncanny way of developing unique marketing methodologies that were fresh and could help specific companies deal with their unique issues in a way that would deliver measurable results expeditiously.

But there were weak points, too, and I saw them. It was like staring into the sun in the midst of a solar eclipse. Painful as it was, I kept looking and thinking and seeing:

- Team members who were at the limits of their intellectual powers and incapable of achieving continuous growth
- Lapses in execution that diminished the power of our collective wisdom

I had to act. I wanted my business, as good and profitable as it was, to be the kind of elegant organism that can move through life with the capacity to grow and evolve and expand and to see through to other dimensions as it finds new sources of knowledge and leverages them. I wanted it to be the kind of company that challenges assumptions and finds the business truths that lie behind them. And then I wanted it to pivot and challenge its own assumptions. To forever dazzle everyone and everything it came in contact with.

Over the course of a challenging but insightful and highly exhilarating two-year period, I took the business apart and put it back together again. The process was painful because I was close to my employees. I liked them. But I instinctively knew that as a manager I had to divorce emotion and friendship from the challenging mission of growing a business.

There was nothing easy about it. Emotions don't simply disappear simply because you wish them away. That magic wand hasn't been invented yet. No such thing as presto-chango, new business. Throughout the process, there were sleepless nights. Cold sweats. I would wake up at 2:00 a.m. wondering if I shouldn't have left well enough alone. Was I playing with fire? Was I jeopardizing what I had worked so hard to build?

There is a line in the film *Wall Street* that goes something like this: "When a man stares into the abyss, he discovers what he is really made of." On these lonely nights, in the midst of the radical change I was imposing on my company and on myself, I knew I was facing my abyss—and that I had to have the managerial resolve to stay the course. I was determined to emerge from the period of pain as a wiser person and a far-better businessman.

My goal was to make MSCO the best company of its kind in the world, but I couldn't do it with the employees I had. I was pushing my people uphill. They were perfectly content to be merely good. But I wanted great. And anyway, managers shouldn't push . . . they should lead. That's a world of difference. Pushers are exhausted trying to make people do what they prefer to avoid. Leaders are exhilarated because they help people dream and turn those dreams into reality.

There's an underlying principle at work here. One that drives to the essence of superior management:

Any enterprise that is equal to the sum of its parts will fail. Only when the components of people, finance, structure, process, morale, strategy, and execution are aligned so that each reinforces the other to create synergy will the organization achieve great things. Because it will be greater than the sum of its parts.

That's what I was determined to achieve at MSCO. And at my clients' businesses. Because the definition of an extraordinary manager is the ability to create and sustain a business unit (of any size or industry) that is greater than the sum of the parts.

Now let's talk about you.

Everyone Manages Something

You're managing your career, your business, and your personal life. And they're all Big Deals.

The question is, do you manage any or all of them well? If you are like most of the members of the human race, the answer is "Not as well as I could . . . or should." And this means you may be failing to reap the full potential—measured in financial, spiritual, and intellectual rewards—of your career, your business, and your life.

Why do I believe that so many people fail to manage their Big Deals with skill and finesse and aplomb? Because I see it over and over again in the course of my work with a widely diverse range of businesspeople at all levels of the management hierarchy. When you are privileged to do what I do, the insights are staggering. I am in boardrooms, helping explain strategy to the board members. I am at their homes, advising on plans to tackle challenges to their leadership. I am at breakout sessions, fielding questions from men and woman stuck on issues that have them flummoxed.

In serving as a mentor, coach, confidante, and personal adviser, I've come to see that many managers exhibit similar weaknesses, finding it difficult to bring themselves to:

- Objectively assess their companies and their management processes. (Ask yourself: Do you really know if you are a good manager? A great one? Compared to whom? To what standard?)

- Conquer their self-doubt (in spite of bold exhibitions of bravado). Think of the times you hate to go into the office because you know quite well that what you have to tell your boss or your team members is weak and unconvincing, and yet you don't know what else to say. So you put on a smile and you stride into the corner office and bam! The worst scenario occurs. Everyone can tell you that you lack the conviction of your words.

- Develop their own management personas (as opposed to choosing role models). I can't tell you how many times I've heard GE managers invoke the name and mythology of Jack Welch. Great for Jack. But they're not him. And you may not be the woman or the man who started your company or the one who held your job before you.

- Make the rules (not follow them). You know how you often wish you could change a dozen dumb rules that have likely governed the company since day one. It's time to put the worst culprits in your crosshairs. Like the Holy Grail at many companies that you can't pay a twenty-four-year-old with one year at the company more than a similarly educated thirty-four-year-old with ten years of seniority. If the kid is a star, PAY her. Wall Street does it every day.

- Smash through the entrenched bureaucracies in their organizations. Everyone knows they are there. Donald Rumsfeld has flown fighter jets and run companies and served as secretary of defense twice. And each time he went to Washington, he had that Department of Defense bureaucracy to deal with. Some factions he left intact (because you rarely want to tear down the entire house), but other cliques of generals learned the hard way (for Rumsfeld and them, because these conflicts are always bloody) that the secretary was driving through their barricades.

- Risk being unpopular in order to become respected and inspirational. I remember when the senior management of Northwestern Mutual Life was under enormous pressure to create a universal-life product in the 1980s. The field force (read: the salespeople who bring in all of the money) was banging down the door for it. But the guys (and they were virtually all guys) said no. Why? Because management believed the product was unsound at the time and, in fact, a time bomb that would implode financially by failing to meet projections somewhere down the road. As the best life-insurance company in the United States, NML could not afford that. So management took the heat from the field, and was about as unpopular as management can be and still remain in office. And then when universal life bloodied the competition, the same "unpopular" guys at NML were the most respected leaders in the industry.

At first blush, the managerial weaknesses cited above may look like a set of disparate issues. But do a flyby at forty thousand feet and you'll see something that may not be visible from the ground: connect the dots, and all of these weaknesses lead to **the absence of a managerial philosophy.**

General Motors puts this in sharp perspective. Here is one of the largest corporations in the world with massive operations and dealerships in everyone's backyard and cars in millions of garages—and what has GM stood for over the past three decades? Lousy cars, eroding market share, roller-coaster earnings, milquetoast management, a trillion rules, and a household name that has as much impact as a blank piece of paper. Through all of these miserable, pitiful, disgraceful years—made even worse by the fact that this company once owned the worldwide auto market—no one at the corporate headquarters has ever uttered the words "Our cars suck." Why? Because all of the managerial weaknesses cited above were embedded in a single company: There were no cold, hard assessments of the company. No determination to tamper with the bureaucracy. No nerve to truly lead by striking out in new directions. No, it was just follow the bouncing ball or the trail of red ink until the neon sign would read GAME OVER. (There are countless GMs out there. They just don't have [in]famous names.)

Which takes us back to this idea of a management philosophy. Don't worry; I'm not going academic on you when I say that you must have one. By "philosophy," I simply mean the framework for what you want to accomplish and how to achieve that. Without a philosophy, you are reactive, responding to each challenge and opportunity you face in random fashion. With a philosophy, you can be proactive, seeing what you face and how you should face it in the context of the strategy you've established.

All too often, managers believe the statement "I want to be highly successful" equates to a philosophy. Not even close. What do you stand for? How will you achieve success? Without a philosophy, there is no path to your goal. No way of dealing effectively with the myriad of issues that will rise up and challenge your intellect, integrity, courage, ambition, and vision.

Tom Watson Jr. needed a philosophy for two Big Deal issues: to prove to his father (founder of the modern IBM) that he was more than just the son of a great business builder, and to take IBM to an even higher level than Watson Sr. had elevated it to. His philosophy was to change the world through computerization and do it on such a grand scale that no competitor could challenge IBM for decades.

The inspiration came on a tour of Metropolitan Life's New York headquarters. The proud prewar building at One Madison Avenue was home to thousands of Met paper shufflers and two massive floors of punch cards—by-products of the state of IBM data management in the 1960s. The new era of mainframe computers was starting to emerge at IBM, university labs, and defense installations—but they were crude, costly, and unreliable. It was at this virtual showdown that Met senior management advised IBM that the company needed to get to the vanguard of computerization: The American business community needed it, and if IBM didn't do it, a competitor would. Floors crammed with stacks and stacks of punch cards wouldn't cut it in an increasingly complex world. At that moment in time, Watson Jr. saw the current market realities (Met was IBM's largest customer) and the future in sharp focus.

When Watson Jr. returned to the office, he had to convince his skeptical father (and his dad's supportive board) that IBM had to pivot away from its astronomically profitable punch-card business and invest unprecedented sums for any company in the history of business to transition to the age of modern, electronic-driven computerization. Big companies don't make radical changes in direction easily, especially when precisely what they are doing and how they are doing it is generating torrents of profit. In spite of all of the resistance he faced, in spite of the fact that he was locking horns with his own father (who happened to be a legend), Watson Jr. stuck to his philosophy and won approval to proceed with the most ambitious growth and investment plan in business history, remaking IBM in front of the world's eyes and creating the first truly great company of the information age. The big bang would come with IBM's introduction, on April 7, 1964, of the System 360: the first major family of computers using a common architecture and interchangeable parts. What *Fortune* magazine referred to as a $5 billion gamble would be one of the most remarkable successes in business history.

In the process, Tom Watson Jr.:

- Objectively assessed his company and its management style
- Conquered his self-doubt as he emerged from his father's shadow
- Developed his own management persona
- Created a new set of rules
- Smashed through entrenched bureaucracies
- Risked being unpopular to be true to his vision/philosophy

Result: He created the greatest company in the world.

Your managerial philosophy need not be complex. Consider mine.

- **I will always have a business strategy.** For example, I don't wake up in the morning wondering what my company will be today or how I will face the issues and opportunities that come before me. They will all be factored into my strategic plan: to keep growing MSCO's ability to see new dimensions and cultivate them for our clients and our business. This impacts my decisions on finance, recruitment, organization, compensation, process, and methodology. My thoughts and actions occur within a strategic/philosophical framework.

- **I will not accept what I am told at face value.** When an employee brags to me, "We are the best at search-engine optimization," I ask who is second best. When he proffers a name, I say, "Bring him in to visit us. I want to see if he thinks we are better than him."

- **I will always seek the truth and base my advice on it.** All of my advisers—including my wife and sons and employees and lawyers and investment bankers—know that I do not want surprises. If the news sucks, tell me as soon as you know it sucks, or, better yet, when you first see it coming. I prefer to deal with problems out on the horizon as opposed to facing them in my conference room.

- **I will not accept second best.** When I know something in my business life falls into that category, I leave the office, put on my L.L. Bean boots, head for the Ward Pound Ridge Reservation near my home in Bedford, New York, and hike alone. And think. And come to grips with the issues. And then I won't sleep until I do my best to move up from the second-best slot.

- **I will not tolerate passive employees.** People who fail to grow are told they are failing to grow; and if they don't get the message, they are fired. If passive people fill the ranks at MSCO, how can I be true to my philosophy, with its emphasis on continuous intellectual growth and the ever-higher levels of performance that go with that?

- **I will not be stopped from achieving my goals.** When I decided to extend my business into China, I was told that the Chinese would not pay for services. Don't waste your time, I was advised. My response: There is always a first time for everything, and people who are too lazy to challenge them propagate half the rules you hear in business. So I found the best China hand in the world to guide me, went into the belly of the beast, and explored a joint-venture business in Beijing.

- **When I am thrown off course by unusual or unexpected circumstances, I will fight to regain my momentum.** It is part of my philosophy that life changes, curveballs are thrown at you, and now and then your world goes topsy-turvy. You lose a big client, a senior employee leaves, a competitor tells the world you suck (as Madison Avenue does to me regularly because they are threatened by my message that big-budget/aesthetics-driven/Clio Award–seeking advertising enriches the agencies and leaves the advertisers wondering, "What the hell happened to our money?"). Unfortunate, sure. But I expect it—and my philosophy says to remember the course of action I have embarked upon and stay the course until that is no longer justified. Madison Avenue hates me because I speak out against traditional advertising. So what.

I'm not going to try to make them my friends. My philosophy says I don't need everyone to like me.

- **I will not be driven by fear.** This doesn't mean that I don't experience fear. I surely do. Fear of failure. Fear of financial risk. But I think about and plan how to protect my downside—to the extent that is possible—and then proceed with my strategy. I know things will go wrong. And I also know that the really successful people, the great managers, lick their wounds and get back on the horse the next day.

- **I will keep learning and growing and connecting to the wiser and smarter me that I can and will become.** Some people say they read three newspapers a day. I made a conscious decision to stop reading any. I recognized that I would learn more by talking to my team members and my clients, hiking with them, holding brainstorming sessions, challenging them, and asking them to challenge me. I ask them all—and I ask it all the time—"I know what we are seeing; the question is, what are we missing?"

- **I will keep passion in my life.** There is only one way to do that: jump with both feet into everything you love. Forget the need to achieve so-called balance. What the hell is that? I love to sit in the sun and dream with my eyes closed. People tell me to beware of the damaging rays. No. It's my passion, so I do it for eight hours or more on a lovely summer day. And I love to drink a bottle of wine every night and two on weekends. Wrong? Unhealthy? No, it's my passion, and it feeds the lifeblood of my life.

I am focused on unleashing the power of a personal philosophy because it is the only way to create and sustain an exceptional enterprise. Note the word "sustain." Creating an exceptional business unit is one thing—and no doubt a very important "one thing"—but the world is full of one-hit wonders that create something special and then watch it deteriorate before their eyes. People who never regain the momentum, the magic, the success of what they achieved at the outset. At a particular moment in time, they had the right product or the right pricing strategy or the right technology to soar from 0 to 100, but they didn't have the philosophy for how to maintain their success and build on it when the inevitable challenges came careening at them from every direction.

Sometimes I meet them at this stage in their evolution. It's then that I set out to discover what went wrong and why—and then work with them to put their business or careers (or both) back on track.

It was that way with Ashley. The daughter of a wealthy Chicago family, she was a classic Midwestern beauty with all-American charm, a winning personality, and a verve for life. A born salesperson, she sold Internet advertising during her summers at the University of Chicago and parlayed her smarts and contacts into a new business that soon thereafter completed an explosive IPO. She had figured out a way to generate high-direct-response rates from advertising dollars, and a long list of companies—frustrated with traditional means of promotion—lined up at her door.

Ashley was giddy with her near-instant success. Perfectly fine: that euphoria is one of the rewards of achievement. But then something happened on the way to a happy ending. The fairy tale turned into a near tragedy. After reaching its high point, her company gradually deteriorated (slowly at first and then, in classic fashion, with increasing velocity) to the point that it was in the red, barely breathing and a candidate for triage. My analysis revealed what went wrong—and why—and now I had to confront Ashley with the facts.

We met on a Sunday in her company's conference room overlooking Lake Michigan. A soft morning sun streamed through a wall of glass. Ashley looked beautiful, her fiery red hair lying gracefully on a winter-white cashmere sweater, but she also had the look of a woman who was not sleeping well.

MS: When you look in the mirror, can you say you have a philosophy?

ASHLEY: I'm not sure what you mean. Am I philosophical?

MS: Do you have a philosophy about how you run your business?

ASHLEY: Of course I do. Why do you ask?

MS: Because you built this place out of nothing but sheer will and pluck and a great gift as a salesperson, but your once and former cash cow is now a broken business veering toward a premature death.

ASHLEY: Oh I know, I know. Times change, Mark. When I started, there was hardly any competition. Today, I've got Google and Microsoft and Ogilvy in my face. What the hell does that have to do with "my philosophy"?

MS: Everything. Times change for every manager, every business. Competition always rises up to show its ugly face. Interest rates rise and fall. Oil prices skyrocket. The stock market tanks. New technologies come out of nowhere. Your best team members decide to move to Maine to write poetry.

Unless you have a philosophy, you cannot manage against all this change. You will fall victim to it. And that is what is happening to you. This business was built on salesmanship. You are an extraordinary salesperson. Everyone loves you. Loves your mind. Loves your passion. Loves the concept you brought to market. And that you quickly built on that by bringing hundreds of Ashleys in the fold, creating a company of salespeople. Of selling machines. Of young men and women clients loved to do business with and who could find opportunity and open doors and close deals. This company showed a broad cross section of American business how to get more bang for their advertising dollars, and they ate it up.

But when the inevitable challenges hit home, you got caught up in dealing with them as one-offs. You mistook salesmanship for philosophy, and no one can consistently sell themselves out of the myriad of challenges every manager faces. For that, you need a philosophy, and respectfully, Ashley, you don't have one.

I could see that Ashley's initial instinct to debate me had passed. Although irritated, she was ready to hear more.

ASHLEY: I see your point. You're right, I have become so caught up in dodging bullets that I don't take time to think where the bullets are coming from and how—in a concerted manner—I can repel them and take the company forward again. That's what you mean, Mark, right?

MS: Exactly.

ASHLEY: If you were in my shoes, what would you do?

Having studied the company's evolution, I was ready.

MS: I would announce my philosophy in the form of a seven-point program designed to turn the business around:

1. The company will reestablish its preeminence in the industry through its founding focus on superior salesmanship.
2. It will regain its high-water mark in sales and revenues—and exceed it.

3. The CEO (you) will lead the drive.

4. You will create a killer offer to romance and reconnect with the customers you have lost and to attract those who have never done business with your company.

5. You will treat the company as a work in progress, getting better every day at sales and strategy and execution and productivity.

6. You will launch an R&D unit to identify the next great innovation in interactive advertising.

7. Nothing will stop you.

Look closely, and you will see that it is more than an action plan: It is a way of thinking and acting that propels business units toward perpetual growth. From that day on, Ashley thought about philosophy in a different way. It was no longer limited to Plato and Socrates. And she no longer viewed her role as CEO primarily in terms of what actions she would take today, tomorrow, and the next day and trust that somehow it would all converge into a plan that would grow the business. For the first time, she created a strategic road map based on what she wanted to achieve over the short and long terms and how she would react and respond to the world whenever the inevitable twists appeared along the road to her goals. She didn't adopt my philosophy: She did something better—she created her own. And within months, the company began to respond to the fact that the leader was

(1) reconnecting with its sales culture by holding monthly workshops and training sessions, (2) enhancing the commission system to provide enriched incentives for landing clients valued at over $1 million, (3) recruiting a senior executive to launch a take-no-prisoners R&D unit, and (4) requiring that her top managers develop and implement their own philosophies for managing their business units under the company's strategic umbrella.

Ashley had come to see the true power of philosophy as a compass for everyone who manages anything. And wants to do it exceptionally well.

How DO YOU KNOW if you have a philosophy for managing? Well, let's think about this together.

Let's start with a question: Do you accept prevailing schools of thought in search of better ways of doing things? Case in point: Years ago, someone advised you that it is not a good idea to "rock the boat," and you may have accepted that as gospel when, in fact, the exact opposite is true. Sometimes you may have to capsize the boat by:

- Tossing out the strategy you inherited

- Replacing members of your team even if (and it usually does) this causes all kinds of political reverberations

- Reengineering the way your business unit manufactures products or delivers services

No doubt, your level in the hierarchy determines the speed at which you can effect change. But the issue is whether you will accept the current state of things as inevitable and thus steer clear of rocking the boat or take on every case of dumb/stale/stupid/illogical thinking (when the time is right) and impose your own philosophy on the way the business is run, rather than allowing yourself and your people to be a victim of it.

The annals of business history are cluttered with *truths* that strong and philosophical leaders challenged and defeated (and, in the process, rocked or capsized the boat):

- Women cannot hold managerial positions.
- Senior people must be more highly compensated than junior people.
- Employees must be guaranteed jobs for life.
- Retail stores need not be open on Sundays.
- It is always better to manufacture your products than to outsource them.

And on and on and on. Think about the way you manage your business unit: Do you challenge tradition in pursuit of greater truths?

Another question: Do you serve as a caretaker or as a leader? I am continuously surprised by how many people with leadership titles serve more as caretakers of their business units than drivers of its strategy/direction/growth.

Caretaking is most transparent in family-owned businesses.

I have worked with the founders' sons and daughters on many occasions. As they take the helm, they tend to look over their shoulders at their mothers and fathers, seeking to perpetuate the accomplishments of those who came before them. Not because what they've inherited is perfect or fabulous or highly profitable. But because it is. That's not managing, that's caretaking—and it's not how you build a great career/business/life. You've adopted someone else's ideas or practices as opposed to creating and deploying a philosophy of your own.

By the nature of their role, caretakers accept traditional thinking. In every case, the wiser course is to challenge it. To hold it under a microscope. To put it through a prism. In some cases, you may find that it has endured for a reason: It is wisdom that has stood the test of time and is still the wisest course. And at other times, you will see it for the imposter it is and replace it with a higher truth.

Case in point: When Bill Levitt decided to become a home builder immediately after World War II, the bible in that industry held that the assembly line wouldn't work there. For cars, yes. Homes, no.

Well, Levitt thought a great deal about the traditional thinking that scoffed at the idea of even saying "assembly line" and "home building" in the same sentence. As a U.S. Air Force officer stationed overseas in the battle with Hitler, Levitt's job was build airstrips for Allied planes on combat missions over Europe. In the war zone, there was no time for the traditional process of planning and constructing runways. Necessity was the mother of invention, and Levitt began to invent new ways to wave a magic wand and have airports appear as if out of thin air. Traditionalists would cry foul, but the Allies needed airstrips and Levitt built them.

And he started to think: I can apply the philosophy of what I am doing here—building overnight airstrips without the bells and whistles of traditional airports—to the home-building process when I return to civilian life. And that's precisely what he did, creating his own version of the assembly line, where the homes stood fixed in place and the workers moved in lines.

Levitt's thinking went like this:

- I will treat homes as mass-produced consumer products.

- I will price them so cheaply that any working person can afford them.

- To accomplish this, I will have teams of workers move from home site to home site, employing their specialties (carpentry, plumbing, etc.) and then moving on.

- I will omit some of the "must haves" of the American home—such as the basement—and this will enable my company to build homes fast and cheap.

This was more than a business strategy. It was a manager imposing a new philosophy on an entire industry. And it created one of the great postwar commercial success stories: the construction of an entire community—Levittown, New York—that still stands as a testimony to the power of declaring war on yourself and the traditional thinking that can hold you in place.

THIS ABILITY TO ENGAGE in zero-base thinking has always been of utmost importance to me. I remember when my boys were seniors in college, about to make the transition from campus life to the business world. I advised them how to tackle what was just ahead.

> *After you graduate from college, you will start a job that represents the beginning of your career. On day one, the company will put a binder on your desk that reads:*

> **ACME MANUFACTURING**
> *Policies and Processes*

> *Study it thoroughly, not with an eye toward blindly obeying everything it says, but instead to look for policies and processes that DON'T make sense, or that are outdated or that you think you can improve upon. Then, when the time comes, POUNCE. Demonstrate to management that you have found a better way. The policies and processes followers will get good performance reviews. You will become their boss. (My sons followed this advice early in their careers. They are young leaders at prominent companies in real estate and private equity.)*

Challenging the Oxymoron of Conventional Wisdom

It was an unusual day at American Express Financial Advisors. A bright young manager—thirty years old, with a finance degree from Boston University—was actually saying something powerful to a team of direct reports.

Unusual because during my many LONG days at this Amex outpost in Minneapolis, the typical banter carried on by members of the middle-management team could be classified as bureaucratic poppycock:

- "Let's demonstrate that we are committed to diversity training."
- "I want you all to make certain that we all collaborate with our teammates."
- "Remember, the most important thing in our business is integrity."

It was enough to make you want to jump aboard an express elevator to the lobby and run as fast and as far from the building as you could.

But today the manager, Owen, was talking about something that had real meaning in the marketplace.

"Our sales force focuses on every market segment except small business. They sell to career executives, housewives, newlyweds, singles, and seniors. You name it and they sell to them—except the biggest market segment of all. The one with the most substantial opportunity. The small-business market.

"When it comes to selling our life insurance and mutual funds, there's nothing *small* about small business. The men and women who own these businesses have mucho dinero in the form of big incomes and high net worth—and we need to claim a bigger share of that pie than the measly slice we now control. We're weak there because our advisers—virtually all nine thousand of them—are afraid of small-business owners. Afraid they will ask them questions they can't answer— questions about cash flow and depreciation and buy-sell agreements—and so they avoid the risk and sell to everyone else, and in the process, bottom line, we lose out. And we have to change that. As an executive in this department, I plan to lead the charge."

But how would Owen lead the charge? He continued to address his team. "Don't get me wrong. I'm not going to micromanage our sales folks. That kind of dot the *i*'s and cross the *t*'s management always backfires. Instead, I want this company to create a training program that teaches our salespeople how to tackle the small-business market without fear—and how to win at it. We'll develop the training; the rest will be up to them."

Why did Owen choose this passive path to address a weakness in the organization that was costing the company a fortune? A path that avoided direct contact with the salespeople. A path that got in no one's face. A path that would take the shape of a document, called a training program, that the sales force (always more interested in seeing prospects than going back to school) would avoid like the plague.

Why? Look over Owen's words. He wasn't about to "micromanage." In other words, he wasn't going to ask the few Amex Financial Advisors who did know how to sell to small businesses to actively mentor their peers. He wasn't going to change the commission structure to skew the sales force toward the most lucrative prospect segment. He wasn't going to tell people who to sell to and hold their feet to the fire if they failed to follow the corporate directive.

Why again? Because that would be "micromanaging," and conventional wisdom holds that to be a terrible thing. A sure sign of misguided, Stone Age management. A straight line to disaster. It's written in stone in every business course and every management text ever created.

 nd it's just one of the reasons I have a bone to pick with wisdom. Yes, wisdom.

How can I argue with wisdom? And what does this have to do with declaring war?

Well, it stems from how wisdom is defined. Just because

something is said to be based on wisdom, that doesn't mean it is actually wise or valuable to the management process. In fact, it may sabotage it.

Consider definitions of "wisdom" taken from *The American Heritage Illustrated Encyclopedic Dictionary*:

Enlightened understanding of what is true or right, usually acquired through long experience, as distinguished from a partial or specialized knowledge.

Accumulated learning; erudition.

The former has value because it focuses on identifying the truth through *enlightened understanding*. Acting on the basis of this visionary truth—painful as it may be or difficult as it can be to divine—is vitally important for sound decision making. And for strong and enlightened management.

The latter definition has more to do with the collection and preservation of information and observations than with accuracy. Think of it as moss accumulating on a rolling stone.

Simply because a fact has been accepted and passed along as the truth for centuries doesn't mean it's true. It is, instead, conventional wisdom, and that may be the furthest thing from the truth.

Precisely because it can become embedded in our brains at childhood, it can be difficult to dispel. And worse than that, we can become inured to the flimsy support underpinning conventional wisdom early on in our lives, and begin to accept the whole concept of conventional wisdom and all of its apparent truths at face value.

Case in point: You know how you were told in your formative years that no two snowflakes are alike. Chances are you heard that as a child and never challenged its veracity. Instead, you found the idea of it thrilling and beguiling. Every snowflake is a unique signature from the sky.

But think about it:

- You don't know if this conventional *wisdom* is true. No one does. No one can. There are a trillion snowflakes in a single blizzard. Has anyone checked to see if they are the same? I don't think so! And here you are—an intelligent person—repeating (and worse yet believing) a cliché that may be entirely false. The question is, does this kind of blind faith distort your business vision?

- Even if Einstein could return to life long enough to prove incontrovertibly that every snowflake is unique, you would be missing another key point. The physical structure of each flake doesn't matter. More important is that combined in a mass of white, cold nature, snowflakes create a formidable presence. Uncommonly beautiful to some; miserable and foreboding to others. In either case, it's the storm and its aftermath that counts most, not the flakes that compose it.

The overriding message of this chapter is to challenge *conventional wisdom*. Look closely, and you'll see that what is often deemed to be the smart thing is actually stale thinking masquerading as the truth. It is a set of assumptions that have gone unchallenged by creative minds for years and gather a presumption of absolute/time-tested/unassailable truth, precisely because they have worked their way into so many minds they are deemed to be fact. But all they've really demonstrated is staying power.

For centuries, conventional wisdom in the retail industry held that the only efficient model for success was to build stores in proportion to the size of the markets they served. Based on this apparently unassailable truth, Podunkville would get a five-hundred-square-foot micromarket and Gotham a football-field-and-a-half-sized big box. And everyone believed this and followed the rules and prayed to the alter of proportionality until Sam Walton stomped onto the scene, did a 180, and put big boxes in Podunkville. By throwing a cream pie into the face of conventional wisdom, Walton did something no one else thought they could do: turned small markets into big markets by using the big boxes as consumer magnets. (Sam Walton wasn't one for conventional wisdom. Nor was Walt Disney when he invested a fortune in Florida swampland and dreamed of turning it into a global destination. Nor was Michael Dell when he was convinced he could compete against IBM—no, beat their brains in—before he had a brand, a single major customer, or a real factory. Nor should you.)

Conventional wisdom builds weak cases around important concepts and then distorts the truth so terribly that managers who get married to convention have little hope of breaking through and achieving breakthroughs. And it's breakthroughs that drive personal and corporate success. Which is precisely why the moss on the rolling stones has to be stripped away and seen for what it is: camouflage.

Case in point: Conventional wisdom holds that great companies, large or small, should make decisions on the basis of consensus. Take it from me. I hear the C-word every day. It's as if God divined it as the bedrock of the managerial process.

Virtually every company I've worked with from Smith Barney to Nike has its own touchy-feely-we're-all-in-this-together way of expressing the alleged importance of consensus building. Boil it down to an amalgam of everyone's C credo and the Holy Grail goes like this:

If teams are assembled to plan initiatives, agree on direction, and identify the means of achieving goals, they will act together to take the hill.

Just the opposite occurs. Here's why: Once a corporate culture encourages and rewards consensus building, the majority of the people in the company or the business unit recognize that the straightest line to success is to conform to prevailing views, as opposed to challenging them. And the prevailing views may simply be those foisted on the business unit by the icons of the past or the loudest mouths in the room. It doesn't matter who is right, who sees the truth, or who can demonstrate its veracity. It only matters that all of the sheep walk together in unison.

You know how often you have said, or heard others say, "I'd like to get consensus on this." But why? And why aren't they (or you) saying, "I am determined to find the truth—the best way to act at this point in time—and to move in that direction, even if those around me think conventional wisdom lays out a safer path?"

When the Japanese attacked Pearl Harbor and the United States found itself in the thick of World War II, Franklin Delano Roosevelt was faced with the brick wall of conventional wisdom. And he drove a tank through it.

Amassed in the Oval Office, the kingpins of the nation's military advised the president to embark on the greatest shipbuilding spree ever conducted. The United States would win the war, the generals and admirals agreed, by commanding the seas. For centuries, wars were won this way. And, according to the prevailing view that bleak December, it was how the new war would be won. Without a doubt.

But Roosevelt knew he wasn't elected to be a shepherd. The American people did not want consensus. They wanted to save democracy. To destroy the Nazis. To vanquish the Japanese. And as FDR thought and listened to brave voices who dared to challenge conventional wisdom, he decided to go on an unprecedented building spree, yes—but of airplanes more than ships. He determined that conventional wisdom had run its course and that contrary to its ardent supporters who advocated naval supremacy, the United States would win the war in the air. And it did. And that single decision was the most significant act in the course of the conflict.

A similar syndrome plays out in business every day. Every minute, in fact. Right now, hundreds or thousands of managers are faced with the choice of basing decisions (big and modest, in giant companies and micro business units) on conventional wisdom or enlightened thinking. The latter is always preferable. What happens when companies get caught in the bear trap of conventional wisdom? They stop asking questions. They believe that because their business model is successful, it will always be so. The folks at Howard Johnson's believed that roadside restaurants offering greasy fried food and a grand smorgasbord of ice-cream flavors would rule the highways for as along as Americans loved to drive and to pile the family into an all-you-can-eat pig-out. Woolworth's execs suffered from a similar form of tunnel vision. The would swear on a stack of Bibles that ubiquitous discount stores presided over by dour spinsters selling a grab bag of bric-a-brac without style or personality or branding would dominate low-end retailing because "Hey, it's worked for decades."

They believed that once consumers move into a certain orbit, they stay there, frozen in their course. Flush with the success of today, it is easy to believe the conventional wisdom that pig-out palaces and dreary discount havens will prevail forever. But let me ask, do you take your family to Howard Johnson's for dinner? When you move into a new town, do you search out the local Woolworth's? Of course not. The sad thing is that these companies (and all the other relics of the past that have suffered similar fates) did not have to shrink into oblivion; they did so because their cultures failed to allow members of their managerial ranks to utter such dangerous (because they would have challenged the status quo) words as:

- "Maybe we should learn from McDonald's."
- "Perhaps people no longer want a food counter in their discount stores?"
- "Maybe the time has come to sell national brands."

Consensus-driven companies remind me of a bathroom joke my friends and I used to share in our Queens, New York, elementary school.

Three stooges are walking down a street. One of them spots what appears to be a pile of dog shit. He approaches it and proclaims:

"Looks like shit."

At which point his friend and fellow stooge bends down and reinforces the finding:

"Smells like shit."

The third musketeer then tops it off by taking his own test and declaring:

"Sure tastes like shit. Man, it's good we didn't step in it."

The fact is that there is no such thing as a consensus decision. It is an oxymoron: a thinly veiled agreement NOT to make a decision. It is a pact that everyone will agree to do the wrong thing knowing that (based on *conventional wisdom*) this is preferable (read: more *socially acceptable*) to a strong and decisive leader standing up and declaring what he or she believes is the right direction to take.

In consensus-based companies, a strong leader acting unilaterally may be perceived as imperious, arrogant, and insensitive. And somehow—to the consensus worshippers— that doesn't seem democratic.

But wait! Companies aren't supposed to be democratic. Corporate decision making isn't supposed to be a town-hall meeting. Great leadership comes when a strong person assesses the facts and decides what to do and how to do it. Consensus occurs when the opportunistic and individualistic drive that makes great companies succeed in the marketplace is replaced by a politically correct culture. And in every company I have ever worked with, I can say with absolute conviction that this culture leads to certain decline and ultimate death.

Forget the horse that looks like a camel because the committee created it. We have heard that too many times. To look at a living, breathing example of a consensus-driven wasteland, spend a day at the United Nations. You'll witness a leaderless, rudderless organization that flounders around spending money and doing nothing but fueling New York's economy (that's one good thing I cheer for at least), thanks to the diplomats' penchant for running up huge tabs at Barneys and Cipriani.

Consensus my ass. The UN agrees not to agree on anything. Has the UN taken concerted action in the Middle East? Has it halted the genocide in Darfur? Does it take an active stance on terrorism? No. No. No. Instead, its members engage in endless debates seeking consensus on complex issues that are not amenable to poetic displays of unanimity. The same is true in the business world. In fact, in many ways, the UN is the mirror image of decision making in millions of businesses. Even if you are a novice manager, you've seen it yourself countless times. It takes a myriad of ugly forms.

- The corporate policy that has been debated for years. (Should we open an office in China? Is it time to outsource those skills we don't seem to be able to master internally?)

- The department head who will not or cannot make difficult decisions and no one forces the issue. (Is it time to replace a supplier who constantly fails to meet expectations?)

- The CEO who insists he cannot make a decision without the support of his senior managers, because doing so would be "bad form."

In the midst of a difficult period at a leading life insurance company, a member of the senior management team recognized that the company was in dire need of new products. The life-insurance market was changing dramatically, and the company was behind the curve in delivering what the sales force (and, in turn, their clients and prospects) were pleading for.

SENIOR MANAGEMENT: I am personally sickened by our failure to generate the new products we need now!

MS: Your competitors—MetLife, Prudential, and Mass-Mutual—are churning them out. Why can't you?

SM: Because my damn new product guy isn't getting his butt in gear.

MS: Why don't you get it in gear for him?

SM: I've tried everything.

MS: How about replacing him with someone who will get this crucial job done?

SM: That would be a problem.

MS: You have a problem now. Three thousand salespeople without a full package of products.

SM: I know. I know. But I can't replace Arnie. All the other senior people like him, protect him, and I can't afford dissension in the ranks. That's not the way to manage a big company like this. Everything is so much easier to do around here when you have consensus.

Easier? Whoever said managing anything is easy? Peaceful? Pleasant? The fact is it's often lonely—and you need to be able to withstand that. Nearly every great company, business unit, or department was and is led by a lion of a man or a woman with a singular vision and the determination to act on it (consensus or not).

Is Steve Jobs a consensus builder? Was Henry Ford? Lee Iacocca? Michael Eisner? Mary Kay Ash? Estée Lauder? No! The only thing these extraordinary managers ever did with consensus building was to pay it lip service, if that. They saw opportunities, marshaled their resources, and acted. And they had to have the conviction and the courage to require that everyone in the business unit follow their lead. Unlike the UN and the IBM of the 1980s and the GM of today, debate has to be terminated and employees (yours, too) have to get behind the manager's strategy. Sure they can offer input, opinions, and warnings—and the manager (you) must be open to all of this—but never with the goal of achieving committee-based consensus. Only with the goal of making iterative improvements in the strategy—and when and if it proves to be ill founded, of changing it.

Consider the people you manage. Conventional wisdom holds they are all unique. That may be true but (like the snowflakes in a blizzard) not provable and completely immaterial. It's how they function as a workforce that matters most to the success of the enterprise. And as a manager, it's your job to see to it that they function like the First Marine Division: They get the job done better than anyone else.

Many of the clichés that distort managerial perception and the decision making that springs from it are based on deeply ingrained misconceptions. As you declare war on yourself and your enterprise, it is vital to attack these misconceptions and address then decisively.

Misconception: Every business unit is a composite of hundreds of strategic and tactical initiatives. The manager's job is to understand them all and be certain they have the resources they need to succeed.

No. The manager's job is to grow the business unit. So while you are busy understanding and being certain and blah, blah, blah, you may be busy as hell while the company stagnates. A Pyrrhic victory, to be sure.

As you declare war, keep in mind the vital importance of

identifying a few powerful forces that can give your business unit exceptional leverage in the marketplace. If you are selling running shoes to Foot Locker, you had better have a sales force that can go head to head with Nike's. Yes, manufacturing and finance and advertising may all be important and all need attention, but the majority of your time and talent should be devoted to recruiting and training and motivating the best salespeople in your industry.

Instead of viewing your business as a composite, view it as a dynamic enterprise whose fate will be based on two critically important levers of growth:

1. Blocking and tackling
2. Breakthrough opportunities

Consider the case of a regional movie-theater company, with the bulk of its screens based in the Northwest. The core of the business is in its operating systems. This means having well-located theaters, in clean condition, showing current films at competitive prices. Blocking and tackling. Get the films, sweep the aisles, and keep the popcorn hot. This formula produces $120 million in annual revenues.

It's the same for any theater chain (and really for almost every business). Once you have the theaters built and the rights to screen major motion pictures (a metaphor for establishing the infrastructure), all you really have to do is open the doors and the revenue rolls in.

So job one is to make certain the blocking and tackling is performed at a higher standard than the industry norm (which is usually abysmal). This means you will want:

- The best selection of movies to screen
- Operating hours that match your customers' lifestyles
- The ability to purchase tickets by telephone and online
- Polite cashiers and ticket takers
- A well-stocked refreshments counter
- Ample parking

By tending to this blocking and tackling with excellence, my movie-theater client was able to grow its revenues about 5 percent per year. Nothing to get Wall Street whipped up about, but this slow and steady component of business growth is critically important. It drives revenue and imposes discipline on the company to conduct itself in a professional, attractive, and competitive manner.

To understand just how important blocking and tackling is to the enterprise, consider the flip side. Once the manager takes blocking and tackling for granted, and assumes the $120 million (or whatever your business unit generates "just by opening the doors") is *guaranteed,* the boat leaks and the $120 million turns to $115 . . . $111 . . . $96 . . . $93 . . . $89 . . . Slowly but inexorably, the company goes out of business.

This was the scenario the company was facing. And yes, blocking and tackling was the culprit. Sloppy theaters, the failure to sell tickets online, surly cashiers, and poor security drove people away, taking ticket sales and revenues with it. In less than three years, a once-healthy company had made the ugly transition from being well run and profitable to going out of business slowly to careening toward bankruptcy.

Here is an all-too-common example of the general manager assuming that because the business was operating well for decades (based in this case on the founder's fervent belief, woven into a needlepoint pillow on his office sofa, that "Profits Are in the Details") it would do so for perpetuity. Once this blind faith replaces managerial discipline, the company veers south. In the theater chain's case, its once-shiny cinemas that promised customers two hours of pleasurable escape became dirty and dangerous. The box office collapsed, and in turn the balance sheet.

Engaged to restore the chain's luster—and, in the process, drive a turnaround—new management focused not on the conventional smorgasbord of issues, but instead on the two big issues: blocking and tackling and breakthrough opportunities.

In short order, they cleaned up the theaters, expanded hours, offered a host of promotions, and made it clear to the world that the dog days were over. The theaters shined, they were safe, they ran hits, and they featured discount promotions for every market segment. In three months, revenues began to rebound. Although dozens of improvements made this possible, they all fell under the umbrella of superior blocking and tackling. The turnaround manager defied the misconception that he had to address 101 issues simultaneously. He recognized that two powerful levers would determine the company's fate—blocking and tackling and breakthrough opportunities—and he viewed every action he took in this context. This way, he could wake up every morning with a relatively simple mission in sync with the overriding managerial mandate to grow the business:

- Make certain my people are executing exceptionally well.
- Make certain we are going to find new sources of revenue.

For the latter, he had to identify strategic initiatives that could lead to dramatic growth:

- Acquisition of competing movie-theater chains
- Diversification into complementary entertainment businesses
- Expansion through investments in additional theaters

Over the course of four years, he moved on all three fronts, most importantly adding theme parks to the mix of entertainment assets. While blocking and tackling continued to grow the revenue base incrementally, securing breakthrough deals more than doubled the company's size and increased its profits sixfold.

Of course, there was far more risk in cultivating breakthrough opportunities than in raising the bar on execution. But the manager took key steps to limit the risks:

- The theater-chain brand was applied to the theme parks, providing instant awareness and a built-in customer base.
- Theme park locations were limited to the Northwest, where the company best understood consumer dynamics.
- Many elements of the theaters' execution strategy were applied to the theme parks.

The fusion of blocking and tackling and breakthrough opportunities creates the platform for a powerful business-building process. Remember, when you look at your business unit, reject the misconception that you must focus on hundreds of challenges or trillions of unique snowflakes and frame your mission in the context of the few levers that have a lopsided impact in the marketplace.

Misconception: The *great* companies in your industry set the standard of excellence. They have mastered the elements of design, production, delivery, quality, and innovation to such a degree that there is little to do but stand in awe and view what they have achieved as *the standard* for growing your business.

Not even close! Take a closer look, and you'll see that the *great* companies in your industry or any other aren't as great as the hype drums them up to be. In all likelihood, they are simply bigger or dressed up in billion-dollar brands. Trading on past glories, they no longer raise the bar on their own performance. Instead, they bask (until the failure to block and tackle catches up with them) in the self-contented glow that comes with the label "Standard of Excellence."

The fact is they leave a huge margin for improvement. But this isn't about lambasting them; it's about rejecting the *conventional wisdom* surrounding big-brand superiority, and instead of imitating them, finding a way to outgun and outsmart them. This provides a springboard to drive the success of your enterprise and your career.

Like every great manager, you need a strategy to distinguish yourself. To build a reputation. To become a hero. A goddam legend. That's how JetBlue's David Neeleman did it. He saw through the misconception of competitive invincibility and recognized that the big guys were really little guys in disguise, more smoke and mirrors than substance—and vulnerable as hell. Yes, American, Delta, and United had:

- More planes
- More routes

- More money for marketing
- More opportunities to shower customers with frequent-flier points and upgrades and free travel

But Neeleman also recognized that they had:

- More surly flight attendants
- More dirty cabins
- More lost luggage
- More food unfit for prisons

So the entrepreneur created a new standard with a series of exclusives fliers would love:

- Free television
- Snacks that beat the pants off standard peanuts and pretzels
- Flight attendants who still know how to smile
- Real bargains without restrictions

In a matter of months, fledgling JetBlue would become *the standard* the Goliaths—even such excellent carriers as Southwest—had to emulate.

Your turn. Start by blindsiding and then beating the Standards of Excellence. You can win by (a) identifying where they stop short of being great, and (b) vastly surpassing the gold standard they supposedly set.

Case in point: Managers in the lodging/hospitality industry will tell you that the Ritz-Carlton and the Four Seasons are the standard setters in customer service. Poke your head into any lodging industry conference and you'll hear speaker after speaker laud these brands as icons because they understand their customer and exceed everyone else at satisfying and retaining them.

The alleged superiority of the Ritz's personnel training is a common theme. No one, it is said, comes close to teaching the staff how to greet and serve visitors nearly as well as the Ritz-Carlton organization. Ever since the great hotelier César Ritz developed his storied service philosophy, "Tell your people to shoot for the moon . . . and if they fall short, to keep trying," the Ritz has had a lock and key on creating the penultimate customer experience. For decades, lodging executives pointed to the Ritz as an extraordinary organization competitors should study and imitate.

What a foolish goal! You don't want to replicate anything. You want to beat the hell out of the competition, no matter how formidable their products or services appear to be from a distance.

Assume we grade the hospitality industry's levels of customer service from A+ to F. The Ritz is widely viewed as setting its bar near the top of the quality spectrum.

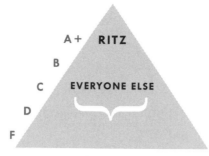

But no. No! No! I have spent tens of thousands of dollars at Ritzes in recent years. I've stayed in suites in their hotels, lost thousands of dollars in their casinos, drank champagne and martinis, and gobbled filet mignons by the dozens. And guess what? The *gold standard* hotelier:

- Never sends a personal note to say thank you
- Never invites me back
- Never gives me anything to acknowledge my loyal patronage

Why? Because like most companies perceived to be gold standard, Ritz's place on the quality spectrum is really here. This disparity between the real and apparent bar settings

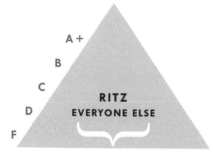

means one thing to business warriors: opportunity. Instead of assuming that the gold standard companies are those you should emulate, view them as those you can and should exceed. Because their bar is set high only when you share their limited view of the potential to surprise, delight, and romance customers and clients.

To wit: Stein Eriksen Lodge is an exceptional ski resort in Deer Valley, Utah. My wife and I have skied and summered there for years. But in spite of our loyalty, Stein has failed to take the time to tell us they miss us and to do something special—like send a limousine to the Salt Lake City International Airport to pick us up the next time we return.

To fill the opportunity gap between the bronze and gold bars, I advised a client in the ski-lodging industry to take a simple but powerful step. When guests are checking out, have the front-desk staff snap a photograph of them (husband's arm around his wife, the couple beaming with the glow that comes from a wonderful vacation). Then presto, this is transformed into a postcard mailed to the customers with the message **"We miss you. Hope we'll see you on the slopes again this winter."**

Just one step in the transition from bronze to gold.

Challenge the misconception that the great companies have all the bases covered, and you'll come up with dozens of ways to raise the bar.

Misconception: It is perfectly acceptable to go to market with a sound product, nicely packaged and well priced. Do this and you have all the bases covered.

No. No. No. No. Take a walk down the supermarket aisles: The shelves are crammed with sound products, nicely packaged and well priced. There's Bumble Bee tuna and Johnson's Wax and Breyers ice cream and on and on and on. But your product may not be there yet; and if it is, it may not be selling well. To achieve these goals (distribution and sales), you must go beyond the basic elements of sound products, nicely packaged and well priced. You must add something to the mix that makes the appeal of the product or service exponentially greater than the sum of its parts. That's because your job as a superior manager isn't to *hope* that customers buy your products or services; your job is to *make sure* that they do. As you make this transition, you must recognize that sound products, nicely packaged and well priced, are simply the cost of admission. It may get you in the door—it doesn't get your product or service out the other end.

What do you have to do to accomplish the latter? When IBM assembled a team to launch what would be a groundbreaking marketing campaign targeted to the small and midsize business community, I advised that we should add firepower to the advertising component by coming up with a killer offer. Everyone agreed. In principle.

Weeks later we're sitting in a conference room at IBM's White Plains, New York, U.S. headquarters, working on the terms of the offer. All eyes are focused on a white board with the words **"Killer Offer"** written across the top. A marketing director and the day's designated keeper of the notes is writing the **Killer Offers** suggested by the attendees.

The problem is, there was nothing **Killer** about them. They were lukewarm/safe-bet/boring-as-hell/easy-to-pass-up deals that people would "stay away from in droves." They ranged from 30 percent off to a lifetime guarantee. Nice to have, but so ubiquitous that they hardly captured attention, in part because it seems everyone makes these offers (and then fails to back them up when you get to the fine print).

Without saying a word, I rose from my seat, moved to the center of the room, grabbed a crayon, and put an X through the word **"Killer."**

Then I explained.

MS: Nothing here is a killer offer. If we don't have the guts or the creativity to come up with one, let's admit it. We can fool ourselves, but we can't fool the marketplace, and they'll be able to tell a milquetoast offer from one that has real sex appeal every day of the week.

A shock to the system the group needed. From there, the meeting moved into fifth gear. When I noted that one of the best offers in New York City provides two Broadway theater tickets for the price of one, Steve—the ranking IBMer in attendance—suggested a twofer of their own. And this evolved into our Killer Offer: For every purchase a customer made of one of the products we were promoting, they could choose another product of equal or greater value for free. And then we would add icing to the cake by handing out 50 percent off discount coupons to the customers' friends and family.

The idea clicked. We didn't drive people to *want* Big Blue's small-business products—software, servers, laptops, desktops, and Internet starter kits—we got them to *lust* after them. Given the economics of the company's business, the freebies not only failed to diminish profitability, they drove it to new levels through cross sales and repeat purchases. The campaign was successful because (a) we changed from the standard IBM techno sell (instead of describing how the servers and the like worked, we focused on how they added value to small businesses), and (b) we created an offer that was hard to pass up.

Misconception: A company's sales culture must be created by its sales manager.

Not at all. It should be created by all of its managers. That's because everyone who works for the business should serve as virtual salespeople. As its catalysts for its growth.

As you think about this, take a page from Manhattan parking garages, the ones run by managers who are driven by the fact that every parking space that is occupied every hour of the day means more dollars in their cash registers. Rather than *hoping* that their garages score high occupancy levels, they hire men to stand on the streets—waving red flags like urban matadors—coaxing and cajoling every car that goes by to come into the garage. They understand that someone who doesn't stop at their garage will pay to park at competitors' garages. So they create a sales culture that permeates the business. Everyone is a salesperson.

Granted, not every business wants to have men waving flags at customers. But the mind-set behind this drive for business should apply to every company. If the most sophisticated radar won't detect a trace of it in the business or department you manage, you have a responsibility to declare war. To change the culture. To turn your business into a selling machine.

When you do so, the math is a thing of beauty.

Recently, I visited a Borders store at the Newark airport. I stopped in to buy a book and a music CD—entertainment for a transatlantic flight. My search turned up an intriguing Philip Roth novel, *The Plot Against America.* Scanning the first few pages, I was mesmerized by the work. When I got to the sales register, a pleasant young woman gently awoke me from a trance. As she accepted the American Express card I thrust at her (my face embedded in the book), she did something exceptionally powerful. She asked me (ever so politely), "Is there anything else you need at this time, sir?"

And then I remembered: I forgot to pick up a CD. Back

into the store I went (the young woman at the register standing sentinel over my Roth book). Within minutes, I scooped up *The Very Best of Sheryl Crow* and was on the way to my flight.

Hidden within this experience lies one of the great secrets to managing the growth of a business.

Let's revisit what happened at that Borders and discover the implications it holds for the company chain-wide and for the business you manage. The young woman at the register was trained to see herself as the Most Important Person Borders' customers deal with. The living, breathing front line of the business. A *salesperson* with an alert mind and a service mentality, she humanized the purchase experience, made the Borders brand come alive, and doubled the gross dollar amount of my purchase.

Which brings us to the scalability of a sales culture. Assume Borders has 1,000 people at its sales registers and that each handles 200 transactions per day. That adds up to 73 million customer contacts annually ($1,000 \times 200 = 200,000 \times 365 = 73,000,000$). Add only $10 of incremental revenue to each sale, and this produces an additional $730 million in revenues.

The moral should scream at you: Even if nothing in their job description has the word *sales* in it, train and reward all the people in your business unit to assume responsibility for *selling* the business. In any way. In every way.

But this is almost never the case.

A leading travel agency relies heavily on its Web site to capture new customers seeking upscale guided tours to the capitals of Europe. So think about this. People hear about the company and get an inkling (based on advertising/PR/ word of mouth/direct mail) that they may want to indulge in this luxurious way to see the world, learn about European history, gain access to private art collections, and experience diverse cultures in a manner that is inaccessible through traditional group tours. So prospects visit the company's Web site and announce—in a virtual way—that they are interested in becoming customers. Sounds good so far, but the story takes a disappointing (and all-too-common) turn.

Instead of doing everything possible to convert the prospects into customers through rapid connection to a travel concierge, the company offers visitors a free subscription to a travel newsletter. A newsletter? The prospects want to hear a human voice, to speak to a knowledgeable person confirming that this travel option is the exceptional experience they are searching for, and to take out a credit card and make a reservation. The company's response: *What's your rush? Read our newsletter first.*

If you are a sales-oriented person, this scenario is hard to imagine. Why wouldn't a company do everything possible to transition prospects to customers? Because so often the managers in charge of the process at the critical junctures are not sales oriented. They see the world through operational eyes as opposed to customer eyes, and if that means making it hard or drawn out for prospects to do business with the company, well, they just don't factor that into their decision making.

Engaged by the client to assess the company's sales process, I asked the editorial director how quickly the newsletter is sent. "Oh, when the next issue is ready." When the next issue is ready! Because no one in the company believed they had a responsibility to serve as virtual salespeople, they were content to allow hot Web site prospects to turn cold as they waited for the newsletter to go through the publishing process. A disturbing anomaly? Disturbing, yes, but in no way an anomaly. This kind of complacency is standard operating procedure at all too many companies. The vast majority of businesses support the conventional wisdom that webmasters, CRM managers, and even customer-service specialists are limited in responsibility to their discrete functions. They don't have to sell anything.

This perspective unintentionally drives prospects into the arms of the competition because the company doesn't go out of its way to draw prospects into a magnetic force field. It doesn't sell. It waits for prospects to sell themselves. Think of that as complacency squared. While the company is taking this passive position, more aggressive competitors are free to pursue potential customers and draw them into their fold. The confidence that prospects will find your offering so irresistible that they don't need to be sold is a false sense of security.

While we are on the subject of selling, let's pulverize another damaging misconception. The vast universe of so-called sales *coaches* will tell you that when you are on a sales call, it's best to tell prospects what they want to hear: that they have a wonderful business, that their lives appear to be in good order, that they should be proud of what they have built or what they own. And so on . . .

No way. Every time a salesperson enters a room, the prospect is expecting to be sold. To be bored. To be manipulated. And then to reject the offer. In fact, they prepare to reject it before the would-be salesperson arrives. And what does the *salesperson* do? Precisely what the prospect expects. He or she prepares an excruciatingly boring Power-Point presentation, stands in front of it, turns off the lights, and puts everyone to sleep. (Who needs Ambien?)

The time has come to declare war on PowerPoint and all the trappings of *tell-'em-what-they-want-to-hear selling.* Instead, use a 180-degree shock-and-awe strategy, jarring prospects with something they never expected to see or hear. Create a pitch or a presentation that surprises them, intrigues them, makes them reexamine the way they think about the product and/or service you are selling. This way you, the salesperson, control the agenda—and that is critical to gaining attention and ultimately making a sale. Once control shifts to the prospect, it is game over. You lose. And forget about making the sale: The prospect eats you for lunch.

Here's how the shock-and-awe strategy plays out in the real world. One of our clients provides a consulting service that promises to improve the efficiency and productivity of manufacturing processes through the introduction of a powerful quality-control methodology. Its competitors—and there are many of them—*sell* on the basis of an engineering-focused-sleeping-pill-of-a-talk that gets into the tings and tangs of manufacturing to microscopic levels. So much so that every person subject to this painful demonstration struggles against an overwhelming desire to lapse into a comalike deep sleep.

See yourself in this picture? As bad as it is, the fact that you are boring people isn't the real issue. More deadly is that you are failing to provide them with a reason—any damn reason—to buy, except on the basis of which vendor offers the lowest-price product or service. Moan as you may about the Wal-Martization of industry, prospects can easily base their purchase decisions on price alone when you fail to offer an intriguing reason to look at anything more compelling than the number of zeros attached to the proposal.

Which bring us back to the need to surprise the prospect. We introduced a new approach for selling our client's consulting services based on the bold (and to manufacturing wonks) heretical statement that **there is no such thing as "modern manufacturing."** In fact, that it is an oxymoron.

As soon as our presentation begins, the prospects (all

manufacturing managers who pride themselves on every single improvement in production processes since the advent of the assembly line) shake their heads in disbelief. In disgust. You can see the steam rising from their heads. You can read their minds. *No such thing as modern manufacturing. What the hell are you guys talking about?*

And now we have them awake/alert/surprised/shocked/ opinionated and demanding an explanation. Then we pounce, broadsiding them with our opinion that the manufacturing process hasn't changed all that much since Henry Ford's River Rouge plant was turning out Model Ts. Yes, techie bells and whistles have been introduced since Mr. Ford reinvented the factory, and yes, products move down the assembly line faster than the steel moved along the Rouge, but basically it's still the same process. In nearly a hundred years, the change has been evolutionary, not revolutionary. We remind them that no one has done for manufacturing what the electronics industry has done for the electric typewriter: turned it into a BlackBerry. With one quantum leap of engineering, the brains behind the BlackBerry took the typed word and whisked it off to anyplace in the world, within seconds. A static process (the clunk of metal and ink on a page) has been turned into an instantly dynamic and magical one as thoughts fly from mind to cyberspace with the BlackBerry's technology. You think and the other party reads. Nothing in manufacturing comes close to that kind of extraordinary change.

This contrast gets grudging attention. And attention leads to discussion and curiosity and the ability to see what is often taken for granted. And when you think about it, that's 90 percent of selling. Now that we have the prospective customer's attention and intensive dialogue has begun, we can make the key points about our client's consulting service:

- That it helps companies view their manufacturing processes through a prism, seeing for the first time all of the steps that can add to or detract from product quality—and how to address them.

- That it is vastly superior to the commodity services that are sold on the basis of low cost. Although our initial fees may be higher, the results are superior, producing a substantial return on investment.

To hell with predictable PowerPoint. To hell with what clients expect to hear. To hell with what they want to hear. Shock them with intelligence! With epiphanies! With the element of surprise! Help them to look at the world through a prism—seeing what they have taken for granted in a new and powerful way—and they will have a high propensity to buy.

And here's another key point: Don't find out what they want! Make them aware of what they don't yet know they want, and need. Glide ahead of the curve by placing an idea/ a dream/a temptation on their radar screens. (Our client did this by making prospects realize that in spite of their thinking to this point, there have been no great strides in manufacturing for generations—and that one is now possible.) If you're talking to them about what they think they already want, chances are they've begun the search on their own. By cleverly employing and leveraging ideation, you:

- Control the agenda
- Take the offensive
- Capture the element of surprise

It's your job to come up with something fresh, powerful, and unique. Rock their boat. Make their day. And yours.

You'll be challenging conventional wisdom and putting your philosophy into action.

Take a Good Look in the Mirror . . .

Do You See a Leader?

Are you a leader? Do you think of yourself this way? Do the people who work for you?

Before you answer, allow me to make a statement that I have found to be true throughout the course of my business career: Unless you are a leader, you cannot be an effective manager. An inspired manager. The kind of person who drives people to achieve more than they would if you were not standing in front of them (as well as by their side).

Now let's delve into this issue a bit more. What if your business card has a leadership title: Supply chain manager. Director of human resources. Marketing coordinator.

All sound as if you are leading something. Ostensibly, you are fusing employees and vendors around the achievement of strategic and tactical initiatives. It doesn't matter if you have one person reporting to you or a small army, if your budget is $10,000 or $100 million—to get the job done, you have to lead. But having the title hardly assures that you are leading. It's just words on a piece of paper. Leadership is expressed in thinking and doing by applying your personal philosophy to the team you manage.

At this point, you may be thinking, "I'm very busy. Without me, this business unit would not get the job done.

In fact, it would be in terrible straits. So I must be the leader in action as well as words."

Not necessarily. Being busy and leading are vastly different. Sure, they may converge, but being busy is hardly the acid test of leadership.

A nd if your business unit cannot get the job done unless you are on the premises, that is generally a reliable indication that something is amiss in your leadership skill.

Strong leaders (and, in turn, exceptional managers) establish a compass for their people to pursue in the course of their work and provide the motivation to exceed established goals.

Can you honestly say you do this? Are you proud of the way your people take the hill? Are you confident that they can get the job done—any job—in a way that elevates your business unit to new levels of success? Or is it just the opposite? If so, you cannot take it out on them. You have just looked in the virtual mirror and come to the realization (perhaps grudgingly) that you are not as good a leader as you can be.

T he time has come to change that. To declare war on yourself. The question is, if you are not a born leader, how can you develop the skills that are essential for extraordinary management?

One thing is certain: Holding a mirror to other people—even those you greatly admire—is not the way to do it. Here's why. As a manager (of your life, as well as your career, your business unit), you've probably looked to emulate role models such as Jack Welch, Carly Fiorina, Bill Gates, Warren Buffett, and the superstar VP two offices down from yours, whose place in the hierarchy keeps soaring along with the success of her business unit. There's certainly a rich pantheon of managerial poster people to worship: the patrician Ivy League executive . . . the street-smart, hard-boiled, self-made entrepreneur . . . the everybody-loves-me consensus builder . . . and lest we forget, the deep, analytical, I-don't-talk-to-anybody-just-get-the-results type leader. And if you are so inclined, you can emulate them all.

It's only natural to want to imitate the stars. To swing a golf club like Ernie Els. To play hoops with the style and swagger of Michael Jordan. To conduct a sales meeting with the electric panache of Steve Jobs. The media encourages this emulation by informing you in colorful detail how these role models make the seas part, earn their place among the managerial elite, and reap harvests of wealth in the process. Surely you've come across managerial profiles filled with all the details you need to try on their personalities, their MOs, like colorful masks at Mardi Gras. You're tempted to do it. Even if these people are cold, driven, cavalier, pompous, and insensitive, the message is that they have the right stuff to make it, and that if you read carefully, you will learn how they do it. And you will be able to imitate them, armed and dangerous.

Completely understandable. And the *worst damn thing* you can do as a manager.

Because you can't pick a persona and make it your own. You can certainly *learn* from successful business leaders. But you can't copy them. If you try, you'll be dazed and confused. A successful manager needs to wake up in the morning and be himself instead of assuming a role that's inconsistent with his personality. His DNA. Sure, I'm advocating that you declare war on yourself, but not to dress in someone else's clothes. Instead, you should keep striving for the full potential that is reflected in who *you* are and can be. If you have been blinded by the hype surrounding the role-model stars, it's time to transition from followership to leadership.

Recently, my company was called on to compete for a major client in the fiber-optics industry. Before flying out for a beauty contest, the prospective client's COO called to prep the key members of my team, focusing on the personalities of the executives we would meet at the company's headquarters when we arrived to make our presentation.

As the COO talked on and on, my radar was telling me that he wanted us to morph our personalities into a multicolored persona that would be acceptable to the eclectic group we would be facing in his company's boardroom. In theory, a good idea. In practice, a prescription for disaster.

MS: Brad, I appreciate your taking the time to give us a lay of the land about your executive team, but respectfully, we can't talk out of two sides of our mouths, much less ten. We are who we are, and we have to be ourselves. I hope what we are meets with the approval of your team.

Real leaders don't dream of being anyone or anything other than who they are. Instead of seeking to copy others, they dream of making something extraordinary happen. Bill Gates dreamed of putting a computer in every office and every home. As I walked alone with Gates on the Microsoft campus in the early 1990s, Bill told me that if he was influenced by anyone, it was Caltech physicist Richard Feynman.

Richard Feynman? I never heard of him at the time, but I did my research soon after. Unusual for a Nobel Prize–winning scientist, Feynman had a compelling way of looking at the world through the lens of a physicist and explaining what he saw in a manner that was understandable and intriguing to the layman. Through this process, Feynman helps his readers see new dimensions in life. He expands their vision by letting them see the *invisible.* Feynman captivated Gates in a way that corporate role models never could.

But Bill Gates is surely an anomaly. In company after company, corner office after corner office, what passes for leadership is really followership. Men and women, corporate executives and entrepreneurs, imitating the icons of business stardom.

Don't go there. Forget about role models and widely accepted schools of thought. You can't be successful following someone else's philosophy, but you can grow as a manager by developing your unique methodology for driving business growth.

By acting on your unique ideas and insights, you will establish an exclusive road map. Your business unit will be different, it will lead and innovate . . . and in the process, it will take the competition by surprise. No one will be able to figure you out, not for some time, because you are painting with colors and brushstrokes they haven't seen before. While others around you are posing as the latest poster person, you are the mystery leader, the individual doing what Gates did twenty-five years ago: emerging and evolving as a unique and exceptional leader. In all these years, it has always been Bill, and his will, and his determination to declare constructive war in search of the next Bill and the next Bill.

Real management success comes from taking stock of who you are and leveraging your capabilities to the moon. True leadership begins by asking yourself what you do well and what you do poorly. This assessment may turn up the following:

Strengths

- Innovative thinker
- Resourceful

- Excellent negotiator
- Strong analytic skills
- Rich and enduring business relationships

Weaknesses

- Wary of new experiences
- Poor at creating a shared vision
- Hyperfocused on execution
- Determined to please superiors

This kind of profile of yourself (the face you see in the mirror, once you are determined to take a hard look) provides a road map for leading with your strengths and, equally important, bolstering the weak side of your balance sheet so that you can grow your leadership skills with a rich lode of personal traits at your disposal.

For example, if you are an innovative thinker, build your managerial model around this. Take your innovative ideas to your team. Not just at meetings but wherever and whenever you can. I know this is one of my strengths so I sleep with a BlackBerry by my pillow. When I wake up with a brainstorm at 3:11 a.m., I e-mail it to my team members and my clients. I do the same at airports and hotel rooms and ski lifts. I am always thinking, I am often thinking creatively, and I know the power of sharing this with the people in my universe. It prompts them to think:

- "Mark is an idea generator."
- "How does he think of these things?"
- "When I need a fresh idea, I will turn to Mark."

Clearly, I haven't cornered the market on creative thinking. And in the light of day, some of my ideas turn out to truly suck. But I am on target often enough to create paths of light for those around me, and they look to this to help guide their actions. It is a powerful leadership tool, and I apply it pervasively.

Glance at the weaknesses list again: "Determined to please superiors." Why is this a weakness? Because it can and often does become Pavlovian. Make a decision. Look for approval. Offer an idea. Look for approval. Hit a sales target. Look for approval. In this constant quest for the acid test of approval by others, you lose yourself.

It happens en masse to entire organizations. Sometimes, the person who makes the loudest call for freethinkers and risk takers is the one who truly wants to hold such people at bay. Why? Because he likes being Mr. Pez, the Approval Dispenser. Like the candy-dispensing device he is named after, he wants everyone in his business unit to compete for approval. He plays an insidious game. Those who dare to express a thought or take an action that runs counter to his thinking are slapped down and humiliated in meetings. At a partners' meeting of the now defunct Arthur Andersen, a tax partner new to the firm accepted an invitation to jump-start the practice to new heights the following year. Rising in an auditorium filled to capacity with his peers, he suggested that the firm begin to sell estate-planning products, such as life insurance, as a profitable adjunct to its traditional tax services.

Mr. Pez pounced:

MR. PEZ: Do you have a license to practice as a tax professional?

TAX PARTNER: I'm not sure what you mean.

MP: Not sure what I mean. What do you find complicated about that? Do you have a license to practice as a tax professional?

TP: Ah, yes . . . of course I do.

MP: Have you ever read the code of professional ethics?

TP: I'm sure I have, and I'm not saying . . .

MP: Then I can only assume that you will be comfortable with this entire firm jeopardizing our ability to practice. OK, Ben, be honest, did you stay too long at the bar last night?

Kick-in-the-face. An assault everyone under Mr. Pez's power learned how to avoid. At the same time, they learned how to win his approval and the perks that went with it. Soon—and this is always the case when a Mr. or a Ms. Pez holds forth—everyone is so busy shuttling back and forth to the PEZ dispenser that they take their eyes off the market. And they pay the price.

The fact is, sometimes what you think or say or do will not be approved by others. They may think it lamebrained or calculating or risk-averse or suicidal, but if you believe in it, you must pursue it without the instant gratification of "approval." Every great manager cares about others, accepts their opinions, and respects their contributions to the business, but does not allow this to become a limiting factor by failing to enact what others may reject. Great managers have the confidence to lead—and that means, at times, going against the grain.

I tell my team at MSCO:

If you think about someone else's motives too much, you are in their heads to such a great extent, they have a right to charge you rent.

Once you liberate yourself from the shackles of what others may think of you, you will be free to soar as a manager and a leader. You'll be able to utilize the full potential of your intellect, drive, and creativity.

But you know something? People rarely do this, because they're afraid of what others may say or think. That they're crazy, inappropriate, or unprofessional. And they will go home having a "bad day" because they had to endure the slings and arrows of the people they pissed off. Pissed off?

Why? Because they took a stand. An unpopular stand. A stand that, right or wrong, earned them ill will. Bad blood. Dislike. But neither they, nor you, should give this an iota of thought. To do so is the kiss of death.

I have thought about this a great deal. I want to be a good man. A good husband and a good father. I want to be a fair and inspiring manager of my company and a leader in my industry. But I don't care if others think I work too hard, or am too driven or demand too much of others and myself. That's me—that's my prerogative—and I'm comfortable with it. I am liberated from renting space in other people's minds by caring what they think of me. This isn't a pissing contest or a matter of pride. It is a way of behaving that is founded in my belief system. I am convinced that leaders have to take unpopular stands because businesses don't grow on the basis of popularity contests. Look at some of my philosophies and tell me if you think my team members "like" me for them:

- When our workload puts us under the gun, there is no such word as "weekend."
- Vacations are the best time to develop innovative business ideas.
- There is no such thing as overworking if you love to work.
- When I have to choose one person over another to

lead a project, I'll take smart and driven over old and wise.

- No one is ever "entitled" to a raise, a bonus, a promotion—or even a job.

Each time I prepare to act on these beliefs, I could stop myself, knowing that people will resent me and will try to galvanize others to demonstrate collective disapproval of my managerial actions. As long as I know that what I am doing is right for the business and in line with my philosophy, I must be oblivious to this. Because if I am not, I will be hostage to it.

As will you. Every way you turn, "the bad day" syndrome can strike. And every place you see it, you have to declare war against it.

Take Southwest Airlines former CEO Herb Kelleher, who walked down the aisles of his planes chatting with his customers and handing out peanuts. His fellow airline CEOs shunned that like the plague. An embarrassment. A step down. Because they thought it undignified, beneath them, or not as important or macho an act such as (in Herb's industry) negotiating a "steal" on the purchase of GE jet engines.

But what Kelleher did was crucial to making Southwest one of the few bright stars in the capital-intensive, zero-margin (if you're lucky), union-riddled airline industry. (I remember financier and former TWA CEO Carl Icahn telling me one night during our weekly tennis game, "The best way to become a millionaire in America is to go into the airline business as a billionaire." Carl was borrowing Virgin Atlantic CEO Richard Branson's line, but he knew the threat of it first hand: At the time, he was struggling to wring a penny of profit out of TWA, the same airline that confounded Howard Hughes.)

Kelleher's big idea grew his business, and all it took to generate that idea was for him to be a leader. The genuine article. A guy who looked inside for inspiration and was willing to take his innovations to the public, to his customers, even if they were untested. While his peers were busy buying jets and romancing Wall Street, Herb was determined to focus every single Southwest employee on the latent power of delivering a unique customer experience. Would Icahn serve as flight attendant for a day? No! Would he hand out peanuts like an hourly worker? No! His ego would get in the way. He would worry about the perception of a Wall Street titan being seen as a waiter. But Kelleher didn't give a hoot. He would do it his way, and he would win at it.

And then, on a somewhat smaller scale (from a corporate perspective), there's my father.

My dad was a supremely gifted salesperson. He was also an avid fly fisherman, and he'd often try to get a little fishing into his numerous business trips.

A couple of times, when I was a kid, he took me along to see clients. He'd say we were going fishing, but his real motive was to show me what business life was all about. I remember going with him to call on a company in upstate New York. We'd been fly-fishing that morning, and on our way to the company I asked my dad where we were going to change out of our fishing attire.

He looked at me as if I'd insulted him: "We're not changing."

We walked right in to see the owner of that company with my father wearing his fly-fishing clothes—I think he still had his waders on, too. I was amazed, but also scared. The CEO was a cardboard patrician who grew up in a dynasty of a family business, had a Tiffany Christmas catalog on the mantle, and probably had (if you can call it that) sex with a tie on. What would he do when he peered out from the inner sanctum of his leather and mahogany office to see my dad and me attired in camouflage pants and angler's vests . . . with worm boxes tied to our belts (just in case the flies didn't do their magic)?

Well, we walked into that church of an office with the grandfather clock ticking and the founder's portrait casting a disapproving eye on the Fishing Jews from Queens and . . . and . . . without hesitation the owner rose from his desk and embraced my dad.

He literally held him in his arms.

My dad's clothes didn't matter, you see. Nor did his name or religion. His personality and business acumen carried the day. What's more, the fact that my father showed up in fishing clothes made him even more authentic and unique to his customer. Consider it a well-kept secret, but customers tend to adore vendors who are bold and sassy and original. Buttoned-up, predictable automatons are a dime a dozen. And everyone knows it. And no one respects it.

The moral of the story? Find your own operating style and make it your signature. Find your dream . . . your will . . . your leadership signature . . . and be true to every element of it. Declare war on every damn cliché you've every heard about the ideal manager and have incorporated into your persona. Leaders aren't made in cookie cutters. They abhor them!

They drive from their DNA. And they say, "My power is in my uniqueness; not in identifying and imitating role models." Do the same! Stop following and start leading. Granted, you can't be a wild man or woman—you need to impose business discipline on your actions—but it has to be housed in who you are and who you can become. Wave good-bye to your peers walking down the road to Imposterville. They'll be working for you.

Recently, I had dinner with Sean, a young manager about to make his first major presentation. Just appointed director of corporate communications, he was on the precipice of the Big Night. The next day he would make his presentation to senior management, outlining his plans for building a corporate communications program from the ground up. This would be the company's initial attempt to build an internal communications pipeline, so Sean had the rare opportunity to paint a picture on a blank canvas. He could shoot for the moon, launching a best-of-breed program that could become *the standard* for the corporate community.

Here was a bright young man about to take on his first major managerial challenge. With it would come the opportunity to demonstrate he had the right stuff. That he was a managerial star in the making. An exciting time, but I could see the unmistakable flash of fear in his eyes.

Was this typical and understandable butterflies or something else? Something troubling? As we shared a steak dinner at Morton's, I decided to find out.

MS: Are you worried about tomorrow?

SEAN: Well, I'm trying not to be, but yeah, I'm worried. But I guess it's only natural.

MS: It is natural to have some butterflies, but is it because you are presenting to management or because you don't have confidence in what you will be presenting? Big difference.

SEAN: A bit of both. I'm not really sure I've nailed this one. My plan, I mean. Can't tell if senior management will like it.

I could read this problem a mile away.

MS: Sean, let's start at the beginning: Do **YOU** like it?

SEAN: I don't know if that matters. I don't write my paycheck, they do.

MS: Yes, they do, but only because they want you to cre-
        ate work that will blow their socks off. They have
        given you a major vote of confidence. You won't live
        up to it by living in fear . . . or trying to please them.
        No, you want to impress them. You want to demon-
        strate leadership.

            Can I have a look at your plan?

It didn't take more than a quick perusal to know that this
was a predictable, cookie-cutter piece of work. It was totally
unacceptable if Sean wanted to demonstrate that he could
join the ranks of the warrior managers.

MS: This plan can't work . . . and I suspect you know
        that.
SEAN: Why do you say that?
MS: Do you think this plan—based on employee e-mails
        and newsletters—will really have an impact on the
        company's morale/motivation/culture? Do you think
        it will add anything of substance to the way people
        work and collaborate with one another?

Sean glanced around the restaurant, as if the answer was
written on the walls. Or perhaps he was searching for the
nearest exit.

SEAN: No . . . that's why I am uncomfortable.

MS: Sean, let me ask you a question that has profound implications now and for the course of your career: Why are you presenting something you are uncomfortable with? Why aren't you staying up all night if that's what it takes to come up with something you are proud as hell of? Something that sings. Something that will change the company instead of assuring business as usual?

Sean stared at me and then blurted out what had been weighing on him for weeks.

SEAN: I know it's mediocre—damn, I know that. But I think this is the kind of plan they are expecting. This is a prudent company that admit it or not likes to stay behind, not ahead of, the curve. That's where they feel comfortable. That's where they perceive minimal risk. That's what defines this culture.

Sean's assessment was correct. Dead on. Bull's-eye. Since the day he joined the company, every message he received from his superiors said, in so many words, "Don't make waves." So his read of the political environment was right, but his plan was doomed to failure. And perhaps his career as well. Think about it: a young manager engaging in followership! A potential star empowered to create a new function and allowed to impose his dreams/will on a blank page chooses to copy what he believes is the norm. The safe approach. An approach that barely, if ever, makes an impact on anyone or anything.

OK, so you're thinking, was he really empowered to impose his will on a plan for a company that shoots free-thinkers between the eyes? Yes. He was asked to create a plan for a new department. Whenever any manager is asked to create anything, he must approach it with all of the passion and intellect he can muster; anything less means accepting the idea that innovators can't succeed. That's equivalent to playing dead.

MS: Sean, don't tell them what you think they want to
        hear, tell them what they need to hear. Yes, there's
        risk in that, but unless you declare war on your fear of
        taking risk, of assuming a leadership approach at any
        stage of your career, you are doomed to third-class
        citizenship.

SEAN: So what is it they **need** to hear?

MS: That hardly anyone has ever done corporate com-
        munications right—with real impact—so your plan
        intentionally violates tradition in order to find a
        code breaker. A way to engage in this process with
        teeth. With results. With power. With substance.

I suggested that Sean ask for a brief extension to present his plan and that we go off-site to brainstorm a fresh approach to corporate communications. One that would discard the clichés and reengineer the process so that it works. Silicon Valley did this. The generation of tech firms that took root in the 1990s eschewed the tired old formula of communicating with employees in print. Gone were the newsletters. Gone were the formal mailings from management. In their place, pizza nights were launched. The members of the business unit gathered in a local dive to share pepperoni pies and Buds and to talk—yes, actually talk to each other, management to employees, employees to management—about everything that mattered to the people or the business or both. This was a novel way to cross-pollinate ideas, to build camaraderie, and, yes, to achieve dynamic corporate communications, in real time, up front and personal.

Dreaming up an innovation like this and putting it into play would demonstrate Sean's managerial genes, but he thought about my offer, politely declined it, and gave the company what it wanted to hear. One thing is certain to me: Sean will soon be just another face in the crowd.

Chances are **you** have been through a similar experience. It is the learning curve in microcosm. You are faced with a challenge, you assess it, and as you look in the mirror, you ask yourself if you have the goods to meet the challenge head-on. As a leader. As a warrior manager.

While you're pondering the issue, try this exercise. Imagine a revolutionary scenario (involving your business) as if it was a dream you had last night. For example, maybe in your dream you sent out a memo that everyone who reports to you could come to work in their pajamas. Or you started a manufacturing division even though your company is in retail. Or you made the sales staff do the bookkeeping and assigned the IT people to sales. Or all internal meetings had to take place in a room with no table or chairs.

Don't hold back; set your mind free just as if you were dreaming. And then, from your dream scenario, choose one seemingly outlandish idea or notion you think can really benefit the enterprise you manage and act on it. Put it into practice without regard to "orthodox thinking/conventional wisdom/the court of public opinion." The only test is that it must have a reasonable chance of succeeding. I like to think of this in terms of *code breakers.* Innovations that will generate opportunities for exponential growth, often by smashing through the barriers that have prevented that level of success.

In one case, I was thinking, "what prevents life-insurance salespeople from gaining access to more qualified prospects?" (The question was important to MSCO, because we represent leading life insurers, and it hit me: the very fact that life-insurance agents are salespeople limited their ability to visit with many of the prospects they would like to see most.

One thing is certain: You can never let fear hold you

back. As it was doing to Sean. And as it can do to all of us now and then.

Let's take a closer look at this fear thing. It is only human for all of us to fear something, sometimes: fear of flying, of public speaking, of making personal commitments, of green-lighting financial investments.

But fear of managing? My experience indicates that that brand of fear ranks right up there at the top of the list. However, it is a quiet fear. An invisible fear. A fear that gets swept under the proverbial rug because no one wants to admit it. To talk about it. To be viewed in any way as timid, weak, vulnerable, cowardly. Fearful.

Still, fear runs deep and can prevent you from exercising your managerial authority in a way that drives your enterprise and propels your career. Precisely because fear is often camouflaged, it is important that we bring it into the daylight and address it head-on.

Let's identify and tackle some of the most common forms fear takes as it seeps into the manager's mind.

I was once brought in to rescue a media business that was hemorrhaging cash big time. The place was a disgrace. It took only hours on the job to see why the P&L statement looked like a B-school case study of what could go wrong—off-the-charts wrong. It was more of an asylum than a business. Discipline was nonexistent. Employees ambled in at 9:30 or 10:00 a.m. or whenever the hell they felt like it, and the place was as quiet as a church by 3:30 in the afternoon. People were at the gym, going to the movies and early happy hours, or at home watching *Oprah*.

The situation with the salespeople was particularly egregious. They were being paid annual salaries of $75,000 just for showing up. If they kicked ass and sold like crazy, all they could do was add 10 percent to their annual comp. Why bother? And they didn't. Just about the only way the company made sales was when clients walked in with a check and said, "I'll take it."

What a deaf, dumb, and blind system. Here's how management's message looked to the people with the title "Sales" on their business cards:

> *Let's tell the salespeople who demonstrate creativity and persistence and drive and determination and a fierce will to win that they will make nearly the same as the slackers in the next office.*

This kind of stupidity doesn't occur randomly. Managers preside over it—or, I should say, *fail* to preside over it.

Why would anyone allow *salespeople* to max out their income without producing sales to bask in the glow of Loserville? To get paid for taking up space? To be called *salespeople* when they couldn't sell anything to anyone?

Fear!

Oh, that word again. It strikes deeper and more often than we all want to admit.

On day one, I entered the scene at the media company as an intruder, an emissary of the owner. The last thing the ruling throng wanted in their midst. For years, they had the license to ruin a perfectly good business. Mostly, because the CEO feared change—and the backlash it would unleash. In my role as acting CEO, I decided to give the sales team an icy shower. Assembling the mod squad in the ninth-floor conference room, I declared constructive war.

MS: I know you're all going to the movies every day. (A sea of faces suddenly turned white.) You've probably seen every movie in Manhattan. Why? Because you've got no reason to hustle. You're drawing generous salaries whether you sell like there's no tomorrow or you don't sell at all. So you pick the destination of greatest pleasure: an air-conditioned movie theater complete with cold Cokes and bags of warm popcorn.

But guess what, folks. Those days are over. History. Your cinematic-enrichment program is still important, but not on company time. From now on, this place is going to be humming. A meritocracy. Have you ever heard of capitalism?

Starting today, nobody goes home early. We're going to work so late that the pizza guy will stop here every night, and we're going to keep at it until we're out of the red and return squarely to the black.

But what I told them next was what truly rocked their worlds. Because it was tangible evidence of my declaration of war, and everyone needed to see the mortar shells fly.

MS: I'm putting a couch in my office. I have no intention of sleeping in my own bed until we've turned this place around. And anyone who is zzz-ing away under a down comforter while I'm holed up in this bunker will be out of a cushy job and on the unemployment line. You can go home at night to your families, but only—only—only if you have done everything possible to drive this business to the next level.

I slept on that couch many nights so that in the mornings when the staff came in (on the nights they felt safe to go home), they would see me in rumpled clothes and know that I'd never left the office.

My wife wasn't thrilled with my new mistress, but I was able to make her understand that it wasn't going to be forever. And in the end, I turned that business around. On the day I left the couch to start sleeping at home again, dinners were still coming into the office via late-night delivery boys. People were working until the wee hours. Complacency had turned into energy. Sales were rising. Movie-ticket sales dropped all over Manhattan. Hollywood had no clue. But I knew.

I shook up the status quo through the symbolism of that couch. In a way words alone could never do, I declared that I was the kind of manager who was going to lead the troops in the charge. I wouldn't ask them to do a damned thing that I wasn't ready to do myself.

And without fear!

Oh, and I was ready to do one thing more, which was . . . I was ready to fire people (when their performance—or lack of it—warranted). To declare war on complacency, to reclaim the business, and face the bad day that would entail as people resented me for upsetting the status quo. And I would keep driving hard until the good days returned, along with the healthy profits and benefits for every member of the team who joined me at the front.

You see, during my tenure at this business, I ended up firing half the sales staff. I absolutely believe in firing people who don't perform, and you'd better believe in it, too, if you want to break free of management that sucks.

Gut check: It's relatively easy to fire the slacker who's bringing down your organization's productivity, but what about firing your star employee? Could you do it? Could you give the boot to your sales ace? When she violates the culture and endangers the business model? How about the person who has your entire IT process in her back pocket?

ould you fire an "indispensable" prima donna on the payroll?

You'd better be able to, because the day you tell yourself you have an employee you can't afford to fire is the day you've resigned as manager and put that individual in your place on the corporate org chart. You've installed a shadow leader!

About five years ago, Richard, the head of a prestigious financial-services firm with over seven hundred employees, invited me to lunch at his exclusive club on the Chicago waterfront, where he dined daily on a fitness lunch of ice water, Boston lettuce, cherry tomatoes, and a platter of sliced pineapple. As we ate and chatted together, I couldn't help noticing that my friend and business associate looked subdued.

MS: You're quiet today. What's disturbing you?

RICHARD: Well, Mark, I have a problem. One of my partners is really scoring big time by landing dot-com clients. He's young, speaks the dot-com lingo, and he really relates to these Internet guys. I'm telling you, in terms of new business development, this partner is a tremendous asset to the firm. A rainmaker extraordinaire.

MS: So far, everything sounds great: a hot partner with a dot-com magic wand. What's the problem?

RICHARD: The problem is that this guy is a textbook schizophrenic: suave with clients, but a real bastard in the office. He's cavalier, arrogant, angry, and constantly making personal demands to feather his bed, to the point that he's throwing my organization into chaos. And when I restrain him—or shall I say try to restrain him—he threatens to take his clients and bolt.

I didn't even have to ponder this one.

MS: If you want my advice, you should put down your knife and fork, end this luncheon now, head directly to the office, and fire him.

Fear!

RICHARD: Fire him? I can't do that—this guy controls so much business that I . . .

MS: If you don't fire him, you'd better recognize the fact that HE'S the new managing partner and you now work for him. Whether he's brought in three hundred clients or three thousand, the question is "Do you want to retain control of your business, or do you want to lose those clients? If you have to choose, which is more important to you?"

Before you answer, remember that he didn't bring in those clients all by himself—he brought them in through the brand and resources of the firm. You've vested this guy with more power than he deserves.

Richard stopped eating and just stared at me. For a minute or so. In total silence. With fear in his eyes. That seemed to turn instantly to resolve. Then, without ceremony, he went back to his office and fired Mr. Hyde. And you know what happened next?

Dr. Jekyll begged forgiveness. He promised, he swore, to change his behavior. He would be a Boy Scout, a team player, Mr. Congeniality. Nonsense, of course, but a skilled manager learns, at any stage of his or her career, how to ping-pong fear back to the bully who backhands it to him on the table. And, usually, the instigator runs for cover. Fear is human, yes, but living in a state of fear never leads to great management. Since Richard's bad day with Dr. Jekyll and Mr. Hyde, the Internet bubble has burst, and with it went the bully partner's glory days. And his leverage. And his power. And his cockiness.

And Richard is still the managing partner. And he is no longer a hostage to fear.

The moral of the story is that when you, as a manager, are faced with a situation that has potentially negative consequences, don't react out of fear. That's management that sucks.

Instead, make certain you understand the risks ahead of time by asking yourself, "What's the worst-case scenario of any action I may take?" Chances are you can accept the worst case, and once you realize that, you've empowered yourself to take action. If your crisis is employee based, (a) change the responsibilities of the employee in question, (b) help the person get outside help if that's appropriate, or (c) ask the person to leave the company. The key point to remember is that whenever the business model goes askew (as in rewarding a renegade out of fear), you must declare war (on your fear) to keep the business on plan and make certain that your authority and flexibility to make the right decisions at the right time is preserved.

Sometimes you weigh the worst-case scenario and have to admit to yourself that you cannot withstand the negative consequences. For instance, say you have an employee who really does have his hands around the neck of 25 percent of your business (as Richard believed about his nemesis). Or that a client who accounts for 70 percent of your revenues is terrorizing you. What do you do then?

You develop a strategy and then implement tactics to get

you out of your predicament. If it's an employee with a stranglehold on your business, you might promote the son of a bitch, kicking him upstairs so that he has to relinquish control of some of his accounts, and then—when the time is right—show him the door. If it's a client, take it as a wake-up call and a long-overdue warning that you can never become dependent on anyone or anything. Appreciate the business relationship? Yes. Value it? Yes. Depend on it? No!

Right now, you're probably thinking that offering such advice is easy. Following it is another matter. But I've been a manager in just this kind of situation many times. Take a close look: I have the scars to prove it.

For example, I know exactly what it feels like to have your business held hostage by a terrorist employee. During that dot-com surge, my company (MSCO) was creating something like twenty-five Web sites a month for our clients. Every company wanted to be on the Web. Most had no idea why or what it would do for their business. But they wanted a Web site. Would anyone visit it? If they did, could the site sell them anything? In the euphoria of the new *Big Thing,* these pragmatic revenue-generation issues didn't matter. Just "build us a Web site" was the lucrative plea we heard every day.

It was during the very height of this cyber gold rush that my interactive director (ID)—a guy who'd only been working for me for five months, and who had the entire MSCO Internet team reporting to him—asked me if I would talk to him privately in his office. And that's when he decided to rock my world. Or try to.

ID: Mark, I'm not in the mood for chitchat, so let me get to the point: You must lend me $100,000. I owe my father that amount, and if I don't pay him, he'll be disappointed in me.

I thought I'd heard it all before!

MS: I'm not comfortable loaning you that kind of money. I don't know you that well. But [I'm thinking that a slew of Web sites are at stake] I'll try to find some way to work this out for you, perhaps by advancing your salary in the form of a loan. So let's sleep on it, and we'll see if we can come up with a way to untangle your financial woes and ease your mind.

It was 10:00 p.m. The MSCO team was working around the clock to get what felt like half the world's Web sites up and running. Millions of dollars of revenue were riding on this, and my ID had much of it in his hands. And he knew it. And so did I.

He responded to my suggestion to sleep on it with a thinly veiled "Fuck you."

ID: That's not good enough, Mark. Either you give me the money, or I walk. I already have another job lined up.

Crunch time. The Big Ultimatum was tossed at me like a hand grenade. In these make-or-break moments, a manager has a second to react.

And I did: I asked my crucial, essential, vital, indispensable, absolutely can't-live-without-him interactive director to wait in his office for a moment, and he grunted, "OK." I went to the supply room, retrieved a supersize Baggie, and returned to his office, where I unfolded it. He didn't know where I was going with this. And then he really got perplexed as I began to remove the personal bric-a-brac from his desk and toss the things—item by item—into the garbage bag.

ID: What the hell are you doing?

MS: I'm helping you pack.

ID: Pack? Pack for what? Why?

MS: You're leaving MSCO. Done. I'm firing you. You're baked. Out of here. No employee will ever hold me hostage.

Poleaxed, he took the bag out of my hands.

ID: You're right. Let's sleep on it, and we'll talk about it tomorrow.

It never came up again.

Yes, I was afraid I would lose an important employee at a time when he appeared to hold all the cards. But I knew that management by fear is management that fails. And I wasn't going down that slippery slope. Sure, I could have handled it more diplomatically: After all, being a politically correct manager is all the rage these days. But it's also one of the big reasons managers often fail to execute on and achieve their agendas.

So I suggest you be politically *in*correct to make it clear to those who work for you that the laws of the marketplace don't allow for psychobabble. They don't give a damn about social agendas. They don't care a whit about feelings. It's all about being the best company, with the best products and services at the best prices. If you don't think that's fair, get a job teaching.

It all comes down to you as a manager creating an appropriate corporate culture, and by that I don't mean a mission statement or some other Hallmarkism taped to the lunchroom wall. I'm talking about the kind of corporate culture that says that the cultivation of an excellent and innovative customer experience (including the development and delivery of cutting-edge products) is job number one, and nobody goes home until that job is done.

Everyone who wants to be successful has to do what it takes! There's no room for political correctness. No one shops at a Target or buys Nikes or eats at Smith's Diner or purchases swimsuits at Jane's Resort Wear because management is kind or fair or protective of endangered species. Admirable traits, of course, but they have zero impact in the marketplace.

Just recently, one of my employees—an exceptionally bright guy with a wife and two small children—came to me and said, "I'm willing to work really hard, but I have to be home every night at six to spend time with my kids . . . because my wife demands it."

Perfect opportunity for me to be politically correct. I could see waves of people, sympathetic to my employees, cheering me to take that route, but I wasn't out to win a popularity contest. I had a business to run.

My response?

MS: You're not going to be able to place your wife's demands before your employment responsibilities here or at any company that cares about the customer experience. Have you asked your wife to envision your life ten years from now (when you'll be facing the prospect of giving your two kids a college education) and to weigh what lifestyle sacrifices you'll be forced to make if you cut back on your career now?

And then I outlined to him the implications of the choice he was about to make. Sending his kids to college could turn into a financial struggle. He and his family might never own the home of their dreams. A comfortable retirement might be a pipe dream.

MS: If you and your wife can accept these facts of life, then you have a meeting of the minds. You won't be working here, but at least you and your wife will be in sync concerning what you want and expect out of life. College may be a struggle and you may be light-years from your dream house, but you are saving two hours of work a day. Sounds like a good deal to her? To you?

I knew I wasn't being politically correct by asking that my employee consider putting work on equal footing with spending quality time with his family . . . and then doing it or leaving MSCO. But before you jump to any conclusions about me, let me assure you that nothing was ever more important to me in my life than being a father to my children. However, because I cared about my career, I took it upon myself to hammer out schedules that allowed me to get the job done in the office and at home, without sacrificing anything with respect to either of these pillars of my life. If that meant working from five until ten on weekend mornings so that I could spend the rest of the days with my boys, that's what I did. Or I would work until 3:00 a.m. every night for a week if I had deadlines to meet and wanted to have the weekend free to take my dear wife and children to the beach.

My eighty-seven-year-old grandmother used to say, "If there's a will, there's a way." Business genius! Also etched in my mind is an episode from the 1950s sitcom *Father Knows Best*. In an unforgettable statement (perhaps only to me), the dad tells his youngest daughter (Princess), "If you ever need help getting something done, ask the busy man. He'll find time to do it." I've always viewed that TV epiphany as a colloquial reflection on Newton's first law of motion: A body in motion tends to stay in motion. (Business genius squared.)

Just between us, I was hoping my conflicted employee—who I absolutely didn't want to lose—would see the light and find a compromise for himself and his family. And that is what happened.

He went home and discussed with his wife the issue of adhering to my corporate culture—whether it would be worth it to them to make concessions to the job—and, in turn, to the hard realities of the marketplace in order to achieve their financial goals. And he came back to me with a request.

"Mark, would it be all right if I stay late three nights a week, and the other two, I go home to tuck my kids into bed and then I'll come back to finish projects if I have to?"

My answer didn't take a nanosecond of thought. "Of course."

As a leader, I had set down the rules, listened to the challenges they posed for my employee, and advised him on a way to navigate effectively through the family and career components of his life. Achieving this balance brought a wonderful feeling of success and accomplishment to both of us.

The problem is that this approach, designed to protect

the integrity of the business (while respecting, within limits, employees' holistic needs), is often jettisoned in favor of that omnipresent cloud of political correctness. Weak managers will tell employees that they can have the time off with their kids every night and accept the fact they will give less than it takes to achieve exceptional success. Or they will say yes to the employees' requests (through gritted teeth) and then begin to concoct poor performance reviews in order to fire the employees on trumped-up charges. Anything to avoid facing the fact that life and business are not always fair or perfectly balanced or infinitely forgiving. Often managers need to make tough choices, and when they fail to do so and opt to sweep the tough stuff under the rug, their companies begin to lose their edge and deteriorate. Precisely the reason why declaring war is more than a "good idea"—it is imperative!

Breaking free of management that sucks requires that you declare war on all of the Boy Scout axioms that prevent you and your business unit from succeeding and instead lead it to a slow, politically correct death.

Sometimes the fate of an enterprise and a career hinge as much on the spirit a leader signals to her organization as the action she takes. The VP of a credit card business unit (we'll call her Jane) appeared to have it all. Big title. Grand office.

Invitation to all the company VIP events. Great setting. But, unfortunately, she was the wrong woman at this point in her career. Let's call her type Ms. Wimp. You'll see why.

She joined the company after a rousing career launch on Wall Street, where she made a name for herself as a bright financial mind who had the rare ability to see the big business picture that surrounds the calculus of spreadsheets and P&L statements. A shoo-in for a top job on the Street, Jane decided to opt for a less-intense working environment and returned to her home state of California, where she joined the credit card company. She started off by knocking the cover off the ball, making headlines by restructuring a number of the company's key banking relationships. Nearly six feet tall, black-haired, and dressed to kill—she favored a line of black Armani suits with an Asian flair—Jane was an imposing presence.

But then an all-too-common pattern set in. I witnessed it this time at an early stage in my business career. Think of it as a *Wonder Years* epiphany. Just as Jane positioned herself as larger than life, as Super Woman, as Ms. Perfect, she took her foot off the gas and coasted. I don't know why this happens, but I have seen it a hundred times since then, and each time the pattern is followed to a T: emerge on the scene, rise like an F-18, level off without rhyme or reason, then descend to the nearest airfield.

As a manager, you must recognize that the expectations

about your performance are in direct proportion to the buzz you create around and about yourself. Make a major splash (and you should always strive for this) and you command attention (something the vast majority of your peers will never do). Now you have a reputation and the expectations that go with it. So if you disappoint, whoa! You will DISAPPOINT. And that usually leads to an involuntary exile to corporate Mongolia.

It appeared that Jane had a strong five-year run at the company, followed by responsible stewardship of her position. But by this point, senior management didn't want or expect responsible stewardship from Super Woman (and they won't from you, either). She bought a weekend house, got into reading the classics, took up bridge—nothing wrong with this—but she also stopped innovating. The ideas that used to fly in all directions like a tennis Lobster out of control vanished. There were private huddles with Jane, talks with the top brass to inquire if something was wrong, and a series of assurances on her part that all was fine and that the senior team would see the former Jane, the star Jane, back at her desk on the proverbial Monday. But the Mondays came and went and the old Jane—the star Jane, the Super Woman—was AWOL.

By the time my relationship began with the company, Jane—the object of considerable and always unflattering scuttlebutt—was regarded as a has-been. Her business unit was in the farm leagues. Yes, as I noted, she was invited to the top-dog events, but only because top dogs need commoners around to bolster their aura of grandeur.

So here's a women on the wrong end of the career trajectory. Even those who reported to her—as well as those like me who observed from the sidelines—viewed her as damaged goods. It appeared that she would hang on for years, read her classics, make excuses, and then fade away into oblivion.

But then a big break materialized. Sometimes it happens: One day a miracle lands in your lap. A layup. How you deal with it has a great deal to do with how and if you cross the winner's line.

Here's Jane's miracle: The president of an important business unit in the company was forced to resign due to financial improprieties (had he stayed, it would have become the business media's Scandal of the Month). Management then asked Jane to step in. Why? She was there, and they needed a quick fix. A body. A suit to come off the bench and pinch-hit.

So it's her big chance. Her comeback in the making. It's a few days before Memorial Day weekend, and she agrees to take on the challenge and pursue the opportunity.

A mentor in the company who had witnessed her rise and fall but held out hope for the return of Super Woman sent her an SOS: Gather all of the managers reporting to you. Tell them to cancel their Memorial Day holiday plans. That you are booking twenty rooms at the Hilton for a month, and they'll all be living there until July 1. Send a clear signal that you and the business unit's team will turn the operations around posthaste.

The "send a clear signal" part of the advice was critical. No one wants to tell people that they have to cancel a getaway they likely need. But business is often less about fairness and balance and right and wrong than it is about power and leverage and reputation. And Jane was lacking on all of those Big Three assets. This was her last chance to reclaim them. Waiting patiently for the day after the holiday would be only a minor delay measured in time but a light-year measured in guts, attitude, drive, determination, and expectations.

Was Jane being advised to make a sacrifice on her part and those of her people? Sure. But not a great one. Her mentor wasn't advising her to go to a war zone. Just to take command and to turn around a troubled business unit—and with that single act, Ms. Wimp would be transformed to Ms. Can Do. Ms. Hero.

And she said, "Thanks for the idea, but no thanks."

Instead, she went on her Memorial Day vacation, let her new reports sunbathe, and allowed a damaged business unit to remain rudderless. Radioactive. What's so wrong with giving a tired staff a well-deserved holiday? Well, first, it was hardly an overworked group, so the no-rest-for-the-weary whine hardly applied here. But more than that, a leader of a troubled enterprise needs to act swiftly, decisively, making whatever sacrifices have to be made to ensure survival, a turnaround, and a competitive posture. But by failing to raise the flag and lead her team into emergency service, Jane failed to lead. And that failure is a major reason management often sucks. Jane needed to declare war on her mañana-will-be-soon-enough approach to business. But she didn't—not at that fateful point before the holiday, nor in the meetings she conducted afterward. Word at the time was that she approached the time-bomb issues at hand in a lackadaisical manner, devoid of a sense of urgency and lacking any of the imaginative touches that were Jane's signature when she built the reputation that she squandered. In the process, she forfeited a platinum opportunity for a center-stage comeback.

Forget about the specific weak-tea steps Jane suggested to her team when they did meet. And about how she proposed to tackle the crisis at hand. Because, as a manager, you must understand that you are judged by a mix of style and substance. Some of the smartest people in the corporate world toil in the bowels of the organization because they are all brains and no electricity. At the high point in her career, Jane was so electric you had to don rubber gloves to touch her. Management wanted to see the old spark again. And if YOU have it, they don't want to see it lose its glow; they don't even want to see it flicker. Imagine the difference if Jane would have gathered the troops at the Hilton, conducted a round-the-clock war room, and presented senior management with a draft of a crisis-management plan before *they* returned from the beach! What she proposed could always be changed, debated, and refined. In this case, when the draft was issued counted for more than what it would say. You, too, will find yourself in this kind of situation. Each time you do, ask yourself, metaphorically, is this a matter of four days, or is it a critical turning point in my career? My life? And then decide if you should take a holiday or book a suite of rooms at the Hilton.

Understandably (anything less would have been near criminal), senior management put out an SOS with Spencer Stuart for a new divisional chief to replace Jane, and the last I knew, Jane continued her free fall into oblivion. Sorry, life can be cruel. Sometimes you ask for it by failing to see that what appears at first blush as big-time problems are opportunities waiting for you to leverage. To do so, you have to stand up and control the agenda (or the agenda will control you).

Think of it this way (politics aside): Harry Truman rose from obscurity as a Midwestern haberdasher to the Man in the Oval Office and left an extraordinary legacy precisely because he took three controversial actions:

- Refused to adopt the conventional wisdom on how to defeat Japan, which favored an invasion by U.S. troops from land, air, and sea. (Even after the existence of the top secret

A-bomb was revealed in Truman's warnings to Japan and the dropping of the first bomb, many traditionalists still favored boots on the ground.)

- Gave one of the most popular and powerful military figures in generations (Douglas MacArthur) his walking papers.

- Dropped the world's first atomic bombs on civilians (to save U.S. soldiers).

Given the choice between fear of criticism and successful management of the war effort, you know what the commander in chief and the thirty-third president of the United States did. What will you do? You know where I stand!

Another case in point: When the scion of a family-owned company took the reins of the business as its CEO, he inherited a superb enterprise with a rich history of excellent products, significant profitability, and an extraordinary customer base. The world, it appeared, was his oyster. All he had to do was take the company to the next level, merely by rising to the role of chief executive that circumstances had dropped into his lap. But it proved to be a far more difficult task than he imagined. As the newly minted CEO sought to fulfill his role, his father—who swore he was the *retired* CEO—refused to step down. Oh, he gave up his title, his parking space, and even his office—but not an iota of power. (Think of guys like Jerry Jones, the owner of the Dallas Cowboys, who prowls the sidelines during games, insisting that he is "just watching.")

Haunting the son, the father made it clear that he (a) founded the business and was its true monarch, (b) knew more about the business than anyone else ever would know, (c) was in the best position to guide its growth, and (d) if his eldest son was going to *manage* the company, he would have to do so by a paint-by-numbers formula set out by his father.

Equally disturbing, the CEO's younger sister—also an executive in the company—believed that it was *she* who should rightfully be in charge. Though she placed second in that race, she was determined to make certain this was but a temporary setback by making her brother look bad/indecisive/ill-suited to run the business. With his father tugging at one side, and his sister snipping like a junkyard dog from the other, the son found himself paralyzed.

His problem was that he was more intent on achieving family peace and popularity than success as a businessman. He would not make decisions for *fear* they would be criticized by his father and his sister—each of whom had different agendas and a poorly veiled desire to watch him drop the ball, reveal his incompetence to run the business, and fail.

Instead of challenging this outrageous situation and demonstrating leadership in the face of adversity, the *CEO* tried to placate his father and sister. At no time did he develop a vision of his own, never mind an action plan for implementing that vision.

In fact, he wasn't truly managing (or leading) anything— not his life, and certainly not the business of which he was supposedly in charge.

It was time to declare constructive war on himself and the business, but the man "at the top" lacked the nerve to do so. After several failed attempts to engage him in strategic discussions on how to wrestle control of the business away from his family and back into his own portfolio, I suggested a course of action that I believed would help him break through the quandary of viewing himself simultaneously as brother, son, and CEO.

Clearly, the time had come for the *CEO*—caught in the parent-sibling crossfire—to declare war on that part of his agenda that was focused on being the good brother and the good son and become a true leader in practice as well as in title.

MS: Take your business card and place it on the night table beside your bed. Every morning as soon as you wake up—even before you brush your teeth—I want you to look at that card and notice that after your name comes the title "CEO." That means you're the guy in charge. The boss. The one empowered to make the ultimate decisions.

As you go through your days, keep reminding

yourself that every move you make must be executed in the manner of a CEO. If that means that you will be dismissed by your father, or ridiculed by your sister, so be it. At least you will be doing the only thing that can help you achieve peace and personal success. You will be fulfilling your role as the company's chief executive officer. You will be declaring war on the forces aligned against you (so what if they're family: sometimes the devil you know is worse than the devil you don't know). You will be managing the business as opposed to managing the voices whispering in your ear (and by the way, trying to deter you from the path of success). There is no reason to fail just because your father and your sister and perhaps a good number of your employees want you to fail. And there's no reason to engage in a popularity contest. You are the company's CEO. Live that role in practice as well as in title and grow the business.

That simple but powerful use of his business card changed the CEO's life. He declared war. He stood up to his father and his sister. He took control. After a half-day huddle in my conference room—at which time we created his management manifesto—the CEO gathered his team and announced the following policy steps, making it clear that they were (1) effective immediately and (2) mandatory:

- All managers must base their day-to-day decision making on the company strategy document I presented to all of you this March.

- Current actions/plans that are out of sync with this must be revised to conform to the document (we can discuss any issues you have relating to this, but you cannot ignore them).

- Any member of the family who requests that you take an action that is new or counter to the corporate policy should be directed to me. (Do not act on any such requests without my express approval.)

- I will be conducting personal reviews with all of you during the following six weeks. My assistant Marcus will provide you with dates shortly.

He is still a brother and a son. But in the business, he is the czar. And that's the way it has to be. Town-hall democracies don't work in the brutal realities of the marketplace.

Let's step back for a moment. You must demonstrate conviction, resolve, determination, courage, and the wisdom to lead. To manage. To harness the power of human, technological, and financial resources to grow an enterprise. Without these traits and skills, the business unit you are responsible for will spin out of control. It will manage you.

This much said, the bravado of leadership is not enough. You need a blueprint to manage against. A compass that guides your actions when you decipher opportunities and when you are tested by adversity. Without this you are a hollow presence. A suit without substance.

One summer I traveled the country with the COO of a diversified real-estate company, which had a major position in the senior-living business. In partnership with Lehman Brothers and other financial sources, the company built upscale independent- and assisted-living residences and then marketed and managed the properties. The company's senior communities dotted the map across broad regions of the Northeast, the Southeast, and the West. Different in architecture, size, and amenities, they shared a common issue: virtually all were operating well below acceptable occupancy levels.

Our mission was to find out why—and to fix it.

As the COO and I made our way across the portfolio of properties, visiting the senior residences and speaking to the managers on-site, I recognized the culprit: It was none other than the company's lack of guidance to the men and women who were charged with profitably running the facilities.

Typical scenario. We flew in the corporate Gulfstream to the West Palm Beach, Florida, airport, where a private car whisked us off to a lavish independent-living facility, the equivalent in style and appointments to a five-star hotel. Handsome buildings, manicured grounds, tropical gardens—

this senior community had it all. Except seniors. Capacity was an anemic 52 percent—far below breakeven. The golden-years paradise was hemorrhaging dollars.

As we interviewed the on-site manager, the COO became increasingly angry and frustrated.

COO: We are spending a fortune on advertising in this market. How many prospects are our ads drawing?

SITE MANAGER: To tour the facility?

COO: What else would I care about?

SM: I only ask because some people call, express interest, and never show up.

COO: Why does that happen?

SM: I haven't the foggiest.

COO: Don't you ever call to see why they don't show up? To ask if you can reschedule a tour for them? If you can pick them up in a friggin' limousine if they don't have a car or are too damn old or dangerous to drive?

SM: Are we allowed to offer that free ride? I've been told that all marketing expenses must—

COO: You've been told to get the bodies in here, for God's sake. [*Trying to calm himself.*] OK, back to my original question. How many prospects visit here a month?

SM: About two hundred.

COO: About? You don't keep records?

SM: It's in my head. No one ever told us to—

COO: And how many of those prospects close?

SM: We have an average move-in of twenty per month. The problem is, about as many either die per month or have to be moved to a nursing home.

COO: So you have a close rate of about 10 percent?

SM: Yes sir, it looks that way. And that's a pretty good average given—

COO: Why do 90 percent walk in the door and leave without writing a check?

SM: Well, we're not in the best location in town and—

COO: Do you think I can move the building? Your job—the one you volunteered to accept—is to fill the building where it is. I can't move it to the ocean to make your life easier!

At this point, the COO stood up abruptly and screamed at the manager.

COO: Goddamn it. I am sick of hearing excuses. This place cost us $25 million and it's a ghost town. You have three months to turn this around. Three months—not a day more.

Clearly upset and frightened by the outburst and its implications, the manager responded to the edict to engineer a turnaround in three months.

SM: How shall I do that, sir?

Once again my client erupted:

COO: How shall you do that? I don't know! I don't have a
        friggin' idea. That's what we pay you for.

At property after property, a similar scene was played
out: hysteria followed by rage followed by a complete lack of
direction.

That's not leadership. It's "screamership." And that does
nothing but antagonize everyone who works for you. Which
brings me back to the need for a blueprint—in this case, one
that would have guided the site managers in greeting
prospects, positioning the property in a way that played to
its strengths (luxurious facilities) and minimized its distance
to shopping malls (by offering a shuttle service), creating a
sales database, developing a follow-up process, and implementing a tenant-referral program. But none of this was
forthcoming because the real-estate/finance guys thought
they could calculate and scream their way to success. They
weren't leaders—they were number crunchers.

His recognition of the importance of leadership—of
moving out from behind the computer and the spreadsheets
and the boardroom meetings to create a brand, a vision, and
a long-term strategy, and to execute on all three with style
and precision—is what makes Donald Trump infinitely more

successful than 99.9 percent of the people who think of themselves as real-estate moguls.

Like him or not, Trump has been a force to reckon with for more than a quarter century—and counting. He is the unquestioned leader of the Trump Organization and of the U.S. real-estate industry. And as he moved along his career continuum from meteoric success to bankruptcy and back again, he has declared constructive war on himself and his people over and over again. From the way he selects properties (location is more important than current physical structure), recruits and retains people (focusing on proven performers and sharing the wealth with them), and finances his deals (he never puts himself at risk of bankruptcy again through personal guarantees), Trump has evolved through the years as the new Donald, and the newer Donald, and the even-newer-than-new Donald. Perhaps louder and more garish, but always rising on the wealth curve.

You can, too. And only you can make it happen.

Develop Your Personal
Killer App

I call it the Nuclear Moment.

It hits my clients with the force of a megaton bomb. I don't like to lob it. They hate to be on the receiving end. But it has to be done. Again and again. Because genteel diplomacy doesn't cut it as the primary ingredient for inspired and effective management and business success.

So the bomb drops.

A good example of a Nuclear Moment in action took place when I was having breakfast in the icy-cool snow-white dining room of a Knightsbridge town house in London, the home of the chief operating officer of a UK-based health-products company. The business was experiencing reasonable growth in line with industry trends, and—emboldened by this success—Kathryn, the COO, was devising her plan to succeed Ian, the CEO, in eighteen months (his recently announced retirement date).

Then I dropped the bomb.

 : Do you think people in the company view you as greater than the sum of your parts?

KATHRYN: [*Clearly surprised . . . caught off balance.*] Let me . . . well, I have to . . . think about that for a moment. Or two.

MS: Don't bother. They don't. Respectfully, they see you as a highly competent manager—skilled in finance, operations, team building—but one who lacks the magic Ian exudes. The something special, something squared, the something irresistible that earned him the CEO's throne. You arrive at meetings armed to the teeth with facts and reports and studies and analyses up the kazoo, and Ian? We know the story, Kathryn. He shows up without a shred of paper. No documents. No research. Nothing to lean on. Nothing the board expects, but something more powerful: a room-rocking idea. A vision that is so compelling and inspiring everyone is hypnotized. They wish it were theirs. They wonder how he thought of it.

Respectfully, Kathryn, you bring credentials to the table; Ian brings the magic of creating ideas. He makes it look as if the ideas struck him as he entered the room, but he plans them meticulously. You see the power of this firsthand—now you have to create a magic of your own. Unless you do so, the board is not going to respect your wish to succeed Ian. They will pursue an outside candidate.

KATHRYN: Well, Mark. I don't really agree. Let me state my case.

MS: Kathryn, forgive me, but business leadership is not about stating a case. That's for the courtroom. We have another goal. To get you to the CEO's office. And job number one is to get you perceived as greater than the sum of your parts. And that's not happening now!

Nuclear Moment!

Time after time I've had to force clients to admit to themselves that they don't have a personal approach that elevates them among their peers and makes them unique. Exceptional. The one to follow (as opposed to the one who is following).

In Kathryn's case, the wake-up call I delivered over croissants and blueberry preserves proved to be the shock to the system this intelligent and ambitious woman needed. At first, she struggled with the message, reminding me that she wasn't Ian (as if I needed reminding) and that she had no desire to be his walking, talking clone at the company.

KATHRYN: Marvelous as he is, one Ian is enough, don't you think? The man's ego barely fits within the walls of Westminster Abbey. I don't know how to nor do I want to imitate the Ian act. My God, it's Shakespearean. Has the man no shame?

MS: Kay, he is the CEO of a world-renowned company. His wealth is in the hundreds of millions of pounds. People adore him—including you and I. Do you think that belongs in the "shame" column?

My point is not that you should become Ian, but that you need to recognize he has developed a style that places an aura, a halo around him. You need to do the same. He may be driven by personality; brains may drive yours. We need to identify a cause célèbre you can rally the company around. Such as the need to focus more on innovation. To be world leaders at it. It's been a decade since this company brought a true innovation to market. Doing so under your guidance would place you, as opposed to Ian, at the epicenter of the universe and demonstrate that you are greater than the sum of your parts.

Kathryn mulled over the issue for months and struggled with it until she made the idea her own. She called me on Thanksgiving night.

KATHRYN: Next Monday, I am presenting Ian and the rest of the board with a proposal to create the Global Center for Nutritional Research. We will own the center and the patents developed in line with our business will be ours, but additional discoveries

will be made available to the nations of the world
on the basis of complimentary licenses.

What do you think?

MS: Genius, Kay. And I hope and trust there will be a clear connection between the center and you.

KATHRYN: I will be its chairperson.

She had it. Although Ian has retained the CEO's seat beyond his announced retirement date, Kathryn is now strongly positioned with the board. Innovations are still a promise, not yet a reality, but the return to the company's research-based cultural roots has helped Kathryn's star to rise, promoted in good part by the founder's family, who together hold more than 30 percent of the stock.

Another real-life Nuclear Moment:

A third-generation family-owned manufacturer of modular buildings was in the blur of a free fall. The failure to declare constructive war through the years had led to the all-too-common slippery slope of a once proud and profitable company sliding backward from growing rapidly to growing slowly to going out of business slowly to going out of business quickly.

How and why did this happen? And what could we do about it?

Before we could recommend the strategy for a turn-around, forensic discovery was in order. But rather than delving almost exclusively into financial documents (the conventional approach in turnaround cases), the MSCO team took an unorthodox course. Based on an instinct (that would prove to be revealing), we reexamined the company's history through the perspective of its annual sales catalogs and brochures. And we discovered something startling. Something numbers alone don't reveal. Something about culture and leadership and the impact they can have on a company's growth or its crippling decline.

Evidence in hand, my executive vice president and I brought our discovery to Benjamin, the CEO. Behind closed doors in his office, I placed the evidence on the table.

MS: We have been looking at how your company has presented itself over the years and, well, we found something quite disturbing.

BENJAMIN: Disturbing?

A perfect gentleman, impeccably dressed and Ivy League mannered—like a character in an F. Scott Fitzgerald novel—Benjamin was clearly taken aback. As if he'd never heard the word "disturbing."

MS: Your grandfather, and particularly your father, were highly creative in the way they positioned the business and sold its products. They broke the rules. They defied convention. While their competitors were advertising in warehouse and distribution trade publications read by supply-chain managers, your predecessors advertised in the high-end architectural and design media read by C-level executives. They hired prominent architects to create buildings with unique design elements and profound character that differentiated your product line from the competition's.

And they went even further, engaging world-class photographers to capture the company's designs in compelling fashion. This artistic approach amounted to a major departure from the industry's cookie-cutter norm—and was thus a substantial gamble—but it placed this company in a rarified space. In a class by itself. The market responded enthusiastically, and the business soared.

BENJAMIN: That brings back fond memories of my summer job days as the boss's son. This place was electric. I felt that when my grandfather ran the business and then even more so when I learned it all on the shop floor by my father's side.

MS: But Benjamin . . . , something happened along the way. Your predecessors saw this as a design business—as an art form. You see it as manufacturing. Do it fast, do it productively, and the hell with art. That may seem like a sound way to beef up the P&L statement, but the artistic sense you have abandoned was this company's key differentiator. Its unique brand promise. All of that has gone—poof!

BENJAMIN: (Blank stare.) Times change. Something always happens along the way. What are you saying? I think you are alluding to something.

MS: Respectfully, *Benjamin,* in the past decade—virtually the entire tenure of your leadership—the "electric" you referred to has disappeared. Sadly, that dynamic quality is now the fond memory of another era. In the years since, there has hardly been a scintilla of creativity or innovation to vest this company with a competitive advantage. Now you play follow the herd: You use hack architects, click-and-shoot photographers, and you advertise along with dozens of competitors in the same predictable distribution/warehousing/logistics publications.

So here's the big question, *Benjamin:* You swerved away from your roots. From your legacy. Why?

Surely, I was challenging Benjamin and forcing him to come to grips with a painful and potentially embarrassing reality. Not to belittle the man, but to help him declare constructive war. To force him to recognize that the way the business was being managed was taking a heavy toll on it, and if left on autopilot, would destroy it.

The message unleashed a tsunami and slammed Benjamin between the eyes. Listening to me intently, he stared at the crystal chandelier above his desk. For what seemed to be hours (but was likely agonizing seconds), he didn't say a word. He didn't flinch. He stared at the chandelier, and when he finally broke the silence, what he said shocked me.

BENJAMIN: I just realized that I've been in a state of depression for seven years! I inherited a wonderful company but had no idea how to put my unique stamp on it. I still don't. I guess that's obvious to you. Now it is to me, too!

Yeow . . . that was more than I expected! A Roger Clemens fastball rocketed back to the mound. At me. At my head. But I asked for it. And I couldn't duck. Didn't want to. Had to face a similar demon when I took the ax to MSCO. As we all must do when we force ourselves to assess what we do and how we do it, so that we can admit the truth and, armed with that knowledge, master the continuum of success.

Certainly, Benjamin's story is unusual in the way the epiphany hit him. But it's not at all unusual in his lack of knowledge as to how to identify and execute a leadership style. The fact is that we all get comfortable in how we do things. We become blinded by habit. But we must recognize this, admit this, and reverse-engineer what we do as managers, asking ourselves each step of the way, can I make a material change that will drive the business unit (whether it is thriving or stumbling) to new heights? The answer is always yes.

BENJAMIN: I started working here as the help. And people who reported to my dad were my boss. When I took over, I let them retain that control. They shot down every idea I had, and I simply gave in. After a while it became a habit. I stopped trying. I was afraid to fight. So I have come in here for years and let the people who report to me, who I employ, not only employ me, but also stop me from being a leader.

I am embarrassed to admit it, but it is so true, it hurts.

In the end, Benjamin rose to the occasion. The epiphany, the depression, and the guilt he experienced on the day of our revelation drove him home from the office a defeated man. But not for long. He absorbed the impact, thought about it, picked himself off the floor, and declared war on his management style, and then on the company. Blaming no one but himself, he roared back, reversing years of lackluster, go-through-the-motions-work with a new sense of energy, creativity, and innovation. He tied back to the company's legacy and made it abundantly clear that those who preferred to resist him this time around would do so from outside the company's walls. He fired obstructionists and saboteurs, he recruited fresh blood, and he drove himself and his team to find new ways to lead the industry. It didn't happen in a day. It didn't happen without pain. But slowly at first, and then with increasing velocity, the company reversed engines and went from going out of business to growing slowly to growing rapidly again.

BENJAMIN AND KATHRYN don't know each other. They never met—but they have something in common. Like you and I (and every manager) at every stage in our careers, they need that something extra, that exponent, that signature trait that will help power their way through the challenges of leadership and arm them with the ability to outsmart/outcompete/outmaneuver/outlast their competitors in their company and their industry.

They need a Killer App.

A Killer App is the stuff the warriors I have worked with have honed to a science. It is their differentiator. It is Teddy Roosevelt's "big stick" and Ronald Reagan's skill as "the Great Communicator." It is why they win. It is how you can win. (No, you may not have all of the traits of the legendary leaders in your DNA, but you can begin to understand where you fall short and make a conscious effort to raise the bar.)

I asked a rising young manager at American Express the same question I asked Kathryn—one that drives to the core of the issue.

MS: Do you think your superiors view you as greater than the sum of your parts?

MANAGER: Well, let me think about that for a moment.

MS: No need to. I know the people you report to. They see you as good, competent, hardworking—but the sum of your parts. No less. No more. And it's in the MORE that the opportunity lies.

MANAGER: What do you mean by "more"? Work even harder?

MS: No. No. No. That's the common mistake. Work smarter. Develop a Killer App. Right now you don't have one.

MANAGER: A Killer App?

MS: Exactly. I know the stars among your peers here. They developed Killer Apps that have defined them and allowed them to be known for something far more powerful than heavy lifting. They are seen as doing sales or problem solving or corporate finance or client charming exponentially better than you and everyone else who has failed to recognize the importance of developing a Killer App.

People who have developed Killer Apps can serve as virtual mentors. When Russell Palmer was running Touche Ross (then the Big Eight accounting firm that would become Deloitte & Touche) his Killer App was focused around team building. Russ knew how to make everyone feel as if they were members of the big Touche Ross family, and that the Touche family was in the league of the Roosevelts and the Rockefellers of families. There he was in his early forties—the youngest CEO in the history of Big Eight accounting—and everyone in the firm felt like Russ's brother. When you run an organization with thousands of people, it's a minor miracle to make your people feel like siblings.

But it wasn't magic. It was smart and pragmatic. To create the illusion of family, Russ worked hard at memorizing the name of every partner and their spouse. When he showed up at partner meetings and greeted all with a "Hiya, Rick and Bonnie, how are the kids?" everyone was in love with Russ. And when he had his office built in an otherwise anonymous Manhattan office tower, he created a private living room where he could talk with partners and staff, congratulate them on their successes, commiserate when they suffered personal setbacks. Russ knew how to work a room. Given that the Big Eight partners voted for their CEO, Mr. Palmer the politician reigned for ten years (before the firm's bylaws required him to retire). He knew what his Killer App was—and how to use it as a potent weapon.

Of course, not everyone can work a room. At the MONY Group—a diversified financial-services company acquired by Axa Financial in 2004—one of the quietest guys in the house had enormous sway over the organization. From the day he walked through MONY's corporate headquarters, this lawyer-turned-tax-genius set out to learn so much about the tax implications of complex financial scenarios and how to structure deals that the folks in the sales ranks couldn't live without him. He worked in a sales organization, couldn't sell a life-insurance policy or a mutual fund if his life depended on it, but he could sell himself—and that became his Killer App. He turned his brain into an asset, a power tool, and because of that many of the monster deals were structured at his desk. He was determined to succeed—in fact, to out*sell* the sales managers—and his driving ambition helped him catapult over an apparent handicap into the winner's circle.

There are four manifestations of a Killer App:

- Monster Ambition
- Cartoon Imagination
- Combat Eyes
- Serial Skepticism

Let's examine each individually.

Monster Ambition

Boiled to its essence, "ambition" reflects the need to *ascend the human hierarchy*. The level of your personal ambition fused with your personal skills equates more or less proportionally to the heights you will scale. It's this fusion that counts. Smarts alone won't cut it.

Think of the smart people you have known who never achieved significant career success. Yes, they moved gracefully through prestigious institutions of higher learning, accumulating academic accolades and advanced degrees, only to toil their entire lives in the backwaters of bureaucracies. If you ever wondered how they wound up there, think of ambition. Or better yet, the lack of it.

An acquaintance of mine—a Stanford B-school honors grad in his eighteenth year of writing compliance procedures for a mammoth life-insurance company—has never had a day of adrenaline rush in his career. Unusually candid and generous, he admits that he has wasted his smarts writing memos no one ever reads and marvels at the extraordinary experiences my career affords me. Learning of an intriguing boardroom battle I was orchestrating on behalf of a client—work that was taking me from New York to the capital cities of Europe and back again, and that was igniting my strategic, creative, and analytical skills— he asked:

ALLEN: How the hell did you get that job?

It didn't take a second's thought to respond.

MS: Allen, I didn't get it. I looked around at the world, recognized that my rather unimpressive college education wasn't going to open doors for me. If I were going to succeed—be engaged in the kind of work that would bring intellectual and spiritual rewards—I would have to create that work myself. So I played with ideas, and the ideas turned into a service, and the service became a business, and the business has grown over the years.

During this entire journey, I have refused to settle. I keep driving toward ever-greater success. I am on that wave of ambition, and I don't envision myself getting off. Ever. This doesn't make me a great person. I'm not. It just gives me one of the great gifts of life: a thrilling and successful career.

Monster ambition is ambition squared. Those who have or develop it can:

Visualize life at the top of the human hierarchy, even if they have no personal experience at that lofty elevation, or easy access to it. Steven Spielberg envisioned himself as the baron of Hollywood when he was still a middle-class kid making home movies in his parents' backyard. There were no connections in the Spielberg family to the famed studio lots built by Warner, Zanuck, and Pickford, but little Stevie could see himself presiding over all of them.

Identify the process or methodology for achieving their vision. Former treasury secretary Robert Rubin came out of the chute determined to be a wizard of Wall Street. But how to do it? As a brilliant young grad fresh out of MIT, Rubin resisted the temptation to view himself as a master of the universe. He knew the Street was crowded with brilliant young grads fresh out of every ivy-covered institution in the world. Bobby Rubin knew he needed more. After accepting an offer from Goldman Sachs, he set out to be the golden boy of the firm's senior partner. Soliciting every kind of assignment he could get from the master, Rubin proved his mettle, made himself invaluable, and rode on his mentor's wings to a partnership position at age thirty-three.

Commit themselves to joining the elite at the apex of personal/professional success. They tell themselves that nothing short of that goal is acceptable. Ted Turner could have easily inherited his father's billboard business, stuffed his bank account with cash, strolled into the office now and then to make it look good, and flown his jet to Montana to ride horses the rest of the time. But none of that midrange success for Mr. Turner. He knew that unless he created a major enterprise of his own—unless he created a network that made his father's look like a school project—he would feel as if he was a sorry excuse for a man.

Monster ambition often takes root through the realization that generally accepted levels of *success*—good job, nice home, and financial security—are not measures of monster success. They are safe imposters, achievable without exceptional drive. Without monster ambition.

Former Disney chairman Michael Eisner put it this way:

> *There's nothing worse than the middle. Mediocrity is the bane of my existence. I'd rather have the most celebrated failure, along with the most celebrated successes, than just a constant life of mediocrity.*[1]

Let's stop here for a moment. I can't tell you how many times I have seen promising people join MSCO, rise like meteors, and then stop in midflight. Done. Dead in their tracks.

Why? Here's a typical example of the conversation that ensues once the juggernaut comes to a halt.

MS:	It seems to me that you have lost your fire. What's going on?
FALLING STAR:	Nothing. I haven't lost anything. What do you mean, Mark?
MS:	Just a few months ago, you wouldn't leave this office until you finished what you were working on. Now you leave in midcourse. And you would be the first one in every morning—not to win an early-bird contest, but to whisk into my office with a new idea that excited you so much, it kept you up at night. That doesn't happen anymore.
FALLING STAR:	What are you saying?
MS:	The fire is gone, and I'm asking why—and where it went. Overnight. Poof!
FALLING STAR:	Mark, work is only one aspect of my life. I have a girlfriend. She wants me home when she gets home. And at her office, everyone leaves at five-thirty. I can't be a workaholic. Not if that means losing the woman I love.

What a distortion of reality that is. It's not that the falling stars are in danger of becoming workaholics, it's that they let people who lack ambition paint them into a corner and hold them back! They tell those who are driven to have a successful career to be one-dimensional. Ambitious and successful people challenge and prevail over that form of pernicious gravity.

I remember when I recognized the need to acquire Monster Ambition. I had graduated from a third-rate college with a useless degree and was living in a tenement in Manhattan. Walking along Park Avenue on a warm spring day, I watched guys in their late twenties and thirties escort beautifully dressed young women into elegant restaurants. I earned $78.50 a week. I was working with *dead* people who lined up for lunch in a company cafeteria at 11:30 a.m. Witnessing the contrast between my current situation and the guys on Park Avenue, I knew I was headed in the wrong direction. No direction, as a matter of fact. Wasting a life. Wasting a mind. That's when I decided to put myself into higher gear.

I did it by employing the process I am suggesting to you. I envisioned myself at the top. I pictured myself as a world-class sprinter before a race—and I never stopped. I remember that when my wife asked me to work less or work mornings so I could spend more time with the children, I did it, and it was my pleasure to do so—but when they tired out, I went back to the office and thought and strategized and dreamed about growing my business, and I did it on Sundays and holidays and in the middle of the night. And I still do. I did it because I acquired monster ambition, and it continues to provide me with an intensity of experience that enriches my life every day in every way.

Mediocre managers are willing to let the ebb and flow of business follow its natural course rather than shaping a business organization to their personal vision. In other words, they let life happen to them rather than grabbing life by the collar and imposing their own agenda on it. Declaring war on it! And that's precisely how their companies or departments (in fact, their lives) slip away to forces that appear to be out of their control.

The good news is that it is never too late to raise one's ambition meter to the monster level. Until he was forty years old, Henry Ford was content to be a mechanical engineer for the Edison Electric Illuminating Company and a tinkerer inventing machines in the basement of his home. Only after his tinkering led to the development of his first vehicle, the Quadricycle, did Ford leave his job to launch the motor company that would bear his name—and claim his place at the top of the corporate world.

Henry Kravis—the son of an Oklahoma oil engineer who rose to become one of the most powerful and influential forces on Wall Street—has always understood Monster Ambition and the role it plays in creating successful managers. As a student and a teacher on the art and science of management, Kravis often lectures students at his alma mater, Columbia University's business school.

In these sessions, he has discovered that what often seems at first glance to be Monster Ambition is just a flimsy facsimile of the real deal.

I ask students at Columbia (I'm on the board), "How many of you want to be an entrepreneur?" A lot of hands go up. I say, "OK, you explain to me what does that mean." "Well, I'd like to go to work at IBM." And I say, "You just failed, that doesn't count. How about you?" "Well, I'd like to work at Procter & Gamble." And I say, "You failed."[2]

Kravis goes on to make a strong point about genuine entre-preneurial spirit and the Monster Ambition that is inexorably linked to it.

A real entrepreneur is a person who has no safety net underneath him or her. That truly has an idea, a vision, and sticks to his/her convictions. You got to have the courage of your convictions. If you did everything by consensus, you wouldn't do anything at all.[3]

Courage, persistence, and commitment . . . these are the building blocks of Monster Ambition. You are proud of your success, at any level, but never, ever satisfied with it. You drive with passion and exhilaration to find the ever-more effective/creative/innovative **you** waiting in the wings. And this assures that whatever it takes to propel the ascending rocket ship of your career, it will get done.

Cartoon Imagination

As we move through life, we are faced with a complex and demanding mix of responsibilities that drive our days and command our time: family, career, social conventions, friendships.

Dealing with all of this forces us to conform to sets of rules, time frames, standards, and expectations that compress our thoughts and actions into tightly constructed patterns of behavior:

- Put the kids to bed
- Respond to e-mails
- Plow through voice mails
- Walk the dog
- Develop a down-and-dirty sales strategy
- And on and on and on

In this way, we fulfill our responsibilities as parents, employees, siblings, friends, and—most important for this crash course—as managers.

On one level, this is the commendable pursuit of duty. But there is a downside. This rush to *get the job done* in rat-a-tat style often restricts the ability to achieve exceptional success. Because the social paradigm forces us to move from task to task, responsibility to responsibility—all within acceptable codes of conduct—it inhibits most of us from engaging in truly creative and innovative thoughts and actions. There is—it appears—no time to think, to ruminate idly, to dream and fantasize. This forces us to engage in ready-fire-aim management.

Exceptional managers are aware of this and are determined to escape the limitations it can impose. They find a way to navigate through the daily conventions to arrive at a spiritual and intellectual free-thought zone where they can engage in unfettered visions of *what could be* as opposed to *what is.* Their thought process resembles doodling; they draw pictures in their minds, and invariably one of those pictures comes to life. I think of this as cartoon imagination.

Is it child's play? Well, yes and no. This way of thinking and living is behind the greatness of Albert Einstein. In our fascination with Einstein's mastery of complex scientific laws and principles, we often overlook the powerful role that fantasy and imagination played in his work. Einstein expressed it this way:

I am enough of an artist to draw freely on my imagination. Imagination is more important than knowledge. Knowledge is limited. Imagination encircles the world. The most beautiful thing we can experience is the mysterious. It is the source of all true art and science. He to whom this emotion is a stranger, who can no longer pause to wonder and stand rapt in awe, is as good as dead: his eyes are closed.[4]

Great managers search for and find ways to transport ideas from imagination to marketplace.

FedEx founder and CEO Fred Smith transformed a blank page and a Magic Marker idea into an extraordinary business. During his student years at Yale, Smith recognized that the world was about to undergo dramatic change driven by the still nascent power of information technology. Based on this vision, Smith wrote a thesis on the sweeping impact computerization would have on society.

When the war in Vietnam broke out, Smith enlisted in the Marine Corps, but he kept a mental picture of his Yale thesis. And it was in the midst of the war that Smith's observation about the future of computerization meshed with the Rube Goldberg reality of the Pentagon's modus operandi for managing its vast supply chain.

Fred Smith:

In the military, there was a tremendous amount of waste. The supplies were sort of pushed forward, like you push food onto a table. And invariably, all of the supplies were in the wrong place for where they were needed.

Observing that, and trying to think about ways to have a different type of distribution system, is what crystallized the idea. The solution was in my mind to have an integrated air and ground system which has never been done. And to operate not on a linear basis—where you try to take things from one point to another—but operate in a systematic manner. Sort of the way a bank clearinghouse does, you know. They have a bank clearinghouse in the middle of all the banks and everybody sends someone down there and they swap everything around. Well, that had been done in transportation before—the Indian post office, the French post office, and American Airlines tried a system like that shortly after World War II. But the demand side and the supply side had really not met an appropriate level of maturation. By the early 1970s when I'd gotten out of the service, it was clear that this new society was coming in earnest. And so at that point, I said, "What the hell. Let's try and put it together."

And that's how Fed Ex came to be.... [5]

In many cases, transporting imaginative ideas from mind to marketplace requires that the successful manager (you and I and everyone at various points in our careers) challenge a self-imposed limitation. This helped propel the career of filmmaker and studio chief George Lucas.

I was a terrible student in high school and the thing that the auto accident did—and it happened just as I graduated, so I was at this sort of crossroads—but it made me apply myself more, because I realized more than anything else what a thin thread we hang onto in life, and I really wanted to make something out of my life. And I was in an

accident that, in theory, no one could survive. So it was
like, "Well, I'm here, and every day now is an extra day.
I've been given an extra day so I've got to make the most
of it." And then the next day I began with two extra days.
And I've sort of—you can't help in that situation but get
into a mind-set like that, which is you've been given this
gift and every single day is a gift, and I wanted to make
the most of it. Before, when I was in high school, I just sort
of wandered around. I wanted to be a mechanic and I
wanted to race cars, and the idea of trying to make some-
thing out of my life wasn't really a priority. But the acci-
dent allowed me to apply myself at school. I got great
grades. Eventually I got very excited about anthropology
and about social sciences and psychology, and I was able
to push my photography even further and eventually dis-
covered film and film schools. [6]

Fred Smith and George Lucas are examples of *dreamers*
who utilized Cartoon Imagination to create powerful business concepts and to serve as exceptional managers capable
of growing important and profitable companies.

This figures prominently into what I refer to as Success
Training 101 at MSCO. When people join my company—and
repeatedly until they get the message/live it/or leave—they
are subject to the following locker-room sermon from yours
truly:

MS: We are in the business of growing our clients' businesses. We can't accomplish that without developing innovative strategies—and those $A+$ strategies aren't sitting there waiting to be plucked. To succeed here—to succeed in life—you have to go off by yourself on a regular basis and THINK. You have to sit in front of a blank page or computer screen and record whatever comes out of your mind. You have to look for powerful new ideas. You have to make time to imagine "What if. What could be. And how to get there from what is."

It's hard to do this because our checklists of chores and endless waves of tactical responsibilities keep us busy e-mailing and calling and flying and lunching and greeting and meeting . . . all to follow the rules and conventions that are part of the fabric of business and personal life. But the winners, the warriors, put a halt to this daily noise now and then and slip into that place where they can imagine. Where they can free-associate. Where they can think from a blank page. Where they can dream. And innovate. And experiment.

When I speak at a seminar, I advise the attendees "not to go back to the office. Not until you have taken one of the ideas you picked up here—one of the principles you learned—and committed yourself to go beyond learning it to putting it into action on the job."

It is so easy for your ideas to evaporate in the heat of the normal business day, one in which you're constantly being called on to answer your e-mail or voice mail or to attend meetings. Unless you make the time to explore, identify, and implement the profound opportunities embedded in your imagination, you will be a mediocre thinker, forever mired in the middle ranks. In so many cases, the determination to engage in imagination is the dividing line between truly successful people and the also-rans.

What side of the line do you live on? Leader or follower? Imagination can make the difference.

Combat Eyes

Carl Icahn earned his wealth and his reputation as a 1980s takeover artist. In the process of wrestling with the likes of such determined corporate adversaries as Texaco, Marshall Field's, and Cheeseborough-Pond's—and in virtually every case intimidating management and securing greenmail, or driving up the price of the stock (and the value of his investment in the companies)—Icahn was labeled as ruthless. To many, his MO reflected the greed of a financial engineer who cared only about his personal gain, even if that put the kibosh on the culture, employees, vendors, and shareholders of his corporate prey. In the heat of the battle, the legion of investment bankers, lawyers, traders, and CEOs forced to lock horns with Icahn have had to ask over and over again: "What does Carl want?"

Invariably, the answer is "More!"

Whether one finds Icahn to be a positive force in free-market capitalism or a pariah abusing the system, it is undeniable that the billionaire raised by a middle-class family in Queens, New York, takes on the Fortune 500 establishment and wins, time and again. How does he do it? Having worked with Icahn, I have come to recognize that the key element in his success is that he views everyone he competes with as THE ENEMY. He distrusts them, expects the worst, crafts a battle strategy for defeating them, and disciplines himself to extract emotion from the process. Instead of acting on the basis of anger or revenge or textbook finance, he bases his business decisions on the principles of the immortal philosophers: Machiavelli, Aristotle, Plato, and Nietzsche. It is through this philosophical lens that Icahn divines his business strategies.

To many, Icahn's modus operandi is ruthless, cold, and impersonal. And it may be. After all, the former Princeton University philosophy major coined the axiom "If you want a friend on Wall Street, get a dog." But his fierce, pugnacious style—whether it is worn on the sleeve or disguised by a more diplomatic and gracious warrior—is at the core of many of the world's most successful managers.

It comes down to this: While the mediocre or incompetent manager is willing to trust competitors, customers, suppliers, and the full cast of people they must do business with until they reveal themselves to be dishonest, manipulative, or unfair because conventional wisdom holds that this is the appropriate way to do business (you are innocent until proven guilty), all of the truly successful managers I have worked with view the landscape with **Combat Eyes (virtually everyone they deal with is viewed as THE ENEMY).**

They are determined to strike first, to strike hard, and to maintain a continuous assault in pursuit of their goals. Trust, fairness, and goodwill, they believe, are for librarians. Their preemptive approach works because while the more passive managers adhere to a code of conduct that restricts their ability to strike before they negotiate in good faith (tradition holds that this is the civil thing to do), the warriors are free to move in any direction, at any speed (good faith is not in their playbook). From their perspective, to do anything else is weak and ignorant and destined to fail.

General George S. Patton Jr. summed up his Combat Eyes philosophy in a fiery speech to the Third Army on May 31, 1944—the eve of the Allied invasion of France:

All real Americans love the sting of battle. When you were kids, you all admired the champion marble shooter, the fastest runner, the big league ball players, the toughest

boxers . . . Americans love a winner and will not tolerate
a loser. Americans play to win all the time. . . .

We're not holding anything. . . . We'll let the hun do
that. We are advancing constantly, and we're not inter-
ested in holding on to anything except the enemy. We're
going to hold on to him by the nose and we're going to
kick him in the ass. . . .

This reflected Patton's principles for declaring and engaging in war:

- Find out what the enemy intends to do and do it first. (You can think of the "enemy" as competitors in and out of your company/business unit.)
- Rock the enemy back on his heels. Keep him rocking. Never give him a chance to get his balance or to build up.
- Engage in relentless pursuit.

If this combative approach to business offends you, sorry to say this, but you will lose time and again to those who prey on your civility. I have never met a successful manager/leader/businessperson who didn't have this combative spirit. Most simply camouflage it with finesse.

I had the good fortune to spend time alone with Clark Clifford—adviser to six U.S. presidents and arguably the most successful attorney ever to hold court in the nation's capital. Elegant, suave, soft-spoken, on the surface Clifford was the polar opposite of Icahn. But was he any less combative? Hell no.

Enthroned imperiously behind the hand-carved walnut desk in his D.C. power office, Clifford—ever the epitome of a polished brass patrician—shared with me some of the secrets and insights of his extraordinary career.

cc: Every lawyer in this town was jealous of my relationships with the men in the Oval Office. Don't you think they wanted to be the adviser Truman called in the night before he dropped the bomb on Japan? Of course, but Truman summoned me. Don't you think they wanted to be the man who had Jack Kennedy's ear when JFK was the most powerful man on earth? Of course, but I had that distinction.

These other lawyers and lobbyists and journalists and assorted Washington insiders would come to me and offer their largesse in helping me define an issue for whatever president I was advising at the time. How nice. How generous. How full of shit it all was. I knew their plan: get in the door on my coattails and build a relationship of their own with the commander in chief. Even belittle me behind my back. And then supplant me. But, but . . . they never got a foot in the door. In the same courtly way they approached me, I was elegant to a fault in telling them, "Thank you, my good sir, but no thank you." The trick is to have the bullshit detector on alert at all times. I could smell a setup a mile away. Ninety percent of the people who call you "friend" are enemies in disguise.

Serial Skepticism

We are all exposed to data, factoids, theories, and axioms ad nauseam. All presented as science, the absolute truth, unassailable. And if you are like most managers, you make business decisions based on this "body of knowledge."

This is where you part company with the warriors.

They recognize instinctively that once any form of thinking becomes "the absolute truth" it is baked, dried up, passé, *fini.*

And then they challenge it. They put it under a spotlight. They examine it through a microscope. This determination to challenge what others accept as the truth (think of it as **Serial Skepticism**) is often a powerful way to achieve breakthrough and sustainable success in your business career. Why? Because while your peers are making decisions based on faith, you are insisting on proof. And that often leads to the truth.

Consider the Serial Skepticism demonstrated by Jonas Salk, the medical researcher who would discover a vaccine for polio and go on to found and manage the Salk Institute. His historic epiphany would come during his second year at New York University Medical School.

We were told in one lecture that it was possible to immunize against diphtheria and tetanus by the use of chemically treated toxins, or toxoids. And the following lecture, we were told that for immunization against a virus disease, you have to experience the infection and that you could not induce immunity with the so-called "killed" or inactivated, chemically treated virus preparation.

Well, somehow that struck me; both statements couldn't be true. When I asked why this was so, the answer was—in a sense—because. About two years later, I had an opportunity to spend elective periods in a laboratory that was involved in studies on influenza. The virus had just been discovered a few years before, and I saw the opportunity to test the question: Could we destroy the virus infectively and still immunize? Through carefully designed experiments, we found it possible to do so. That was how a particular line of investigation occurred—and it influenced my career.

I just didn't accept what appeared to be a dogmatic assertion in view of the fact that there was reason to think otherwise.[7]

Adopting Serial Skepticism requires that you make the critical transition from accepting most of what you hear and learn as fact to viewing this input as:

- A possibility that still must be proven
- A lie designed to enhance the position of the party providing the input
- A school of thought or a standard of practice that has been accepted as the gospel for years, perhaps for generations, but whose credibility is based on blind faith

As you seek to incorporate Serial Skepticism into your managerial process and employ it to develop your Killer App, take the following steps:

- When you are assigned to conduct any task according to a prescribed method, ask yourself if there is a better way of performing the activity.

- If you are inclined to trust someone's information, intentions, or motives, ask yourself if he will gain more by misleading you than by sharing his knowledge. Remember: Your goals and the goals of *advisers* may be dramatically opposite. Case in point: They may want you to buy something from them (software, consulting, etc.) that may have little benefit besides earning the *adviser* commissions.

- When someone makes a purported statement of *fact,* ask yourself if it is really fact or fantasy. And demand of yourself (as well as your employees, vendors, bankers, and advisers) that the *fact* be proven.

One of the best ways to create a powerful personal presence (to be viewed as more than the sum of your parts) is to develop a reputation in the company for being a bulldog for the truth by using Serial Skepticism—and the guts to act on it—to drive your business unit out of the comfort zone of conventional but erroneous thinking. This quixotic approach to intellect and execution is at the intersection where truth and opportunity converge.

Your crash-course mission is to identify where the Killer App(s) you can adopt and the needs of the business unit you manage converge. It's the surefire way to build something of substance and to race ahead of your peers—most of whom don't understand it's a race or don't know how to run it. To win it.

Unleashing Your
Manhattan Project

The Plan That Will

Change Your

World . . . and

Your Life

Nearly two years before the United States entered World War II, President Franklin Roosevelt authorized a top secret plan to vanquish the enemy. To win the battle hands down. Complete and total victory.

Roosevelt's audacious move called for a team of leading physicists led by Robert Oppenheimer to develop the world's first atomic bomb. Known as the Manhattan Project (formally, the Manhattan Engineering District), the program was originally centered under a squash court at the University of Chicago. Working in a race against time (Roosevelt knew that the Nazis were also working on an atomic bomb), the Manhattan Project resulted in the production of three nuclear weapons: the first tested near Alamogordo, New Mexico, and the second and third dropped on the Japanese cities of Hiroshima and Nagasaki, ending the war with Japan.

The Manhattan Project led to a momentous turning point in history. This is not the place to examine how and why it worked, except that it was the by-product of exceptional vision and decisive leadership. Similarly—if to a lesser extent—the best managers are visionary and decisive. Eagles. Agenda-setting warriors guided by extraordinary battle plans.

Case in point: When Ronald Reagan assumed the presidency of the United States, he announced a one-hundred-day plan that would:

- Reduce income taxes
- Dramatically rebuild the military and seek to end the Cold War
- Diminish the power of the labor unions

Forget your view of Reagan's politics. View his bold plan in a business context. In effect, he declared war on the United States, believing (many now say *demonstrating*) that a frontal attack conducted in a tight and defined time frame on established practices and organizations would make the nation stronger.

Fast forward to the corporate front. If a company ever needed to have war declared on itself, it was the IBM of the early 1990s. With losses mounting into the billions, the giant that had long reigned as the model of corporate excellence was skidding along the reverse trajectory from fast growth to slow growth to going out of business slowly to going out of business rapidly.

Just when a badly humbled Big Blue needed to muster all of the energy, talent, ambition, drive, and sheer will of its people to bring it back from the brink, the spoiled technocrats in charge of the bloated IBM bureaucracy locked the doors to their offices and waited for the storm to pass. As if life is that easy. As if crippled companies magically heal themselves. As if a fairy godmother waves a wand and gold dust descends from the heavens.

Visiting the company's U.S. headquarters during that dark and depressing period, I found a dearth of ideas, concern, urgency, accountability, and commitment. It was as if nothing had changed since IBM exploded on the scene at the vanguard of the IT revolution. To almost everyone at IBM during this sorry state in its history, everything was just fine. Life was a long lunch hour. The checks would keep coming.

A national treasure was going down the tubes, and no one seemed to care. And then, just as the business was about to implode, the board took its head out of the sand, got off its ass, and acted, installing an unlikely savior in the person of Lou Gerstner. A packaged-goods guy who knew next to nothing about technology, Gerstner appeared to be the perfect clay pigeon for the losers who had pushed the company into an abyss. They would embarrass him into submission, reclaim the company, and ride out their paychecks for as long as they lasted. Why deal with reality now? They hadn't done so for a decade. Nothing, they believed, was really going to change.

And then Gerstner rode into town. And he proved from day one that he was a man with a plan. And the guts to carry it out.

The old guard advised Gerstner that creating a new mission statement should be his top priority. Job one. Absolutely essential. Life and death for the new IBM. But Big Lou made it clear it was *not* business as usual at the new IBM. No, he would not create a new mission statement because he knew (as did everyone who ever worked for or with IBM—including yours truly) that the bureaucracy would debate it to a pulp and never act on it anyway. He preferred to get into the market and reconnect with IBM's historic (but now abandoned) focus on sales.

A shot across the bow. The opening salvo of Gerstner's war on the company he inherited. He would face the truth and admit failure: IBMers talked to one another too much. Lived in PowerPoint Land. Attended a zillion meetings. Accomplished nothing and didn't give a damn that they had nothing to show for their work but red ink. Now that chapter was over. Done. History.

Gerstner's Manhattan Project was focused on cracking the code IBM could deploy to once again dominate the IT market. He needed his own nuclear bomb to demonstrate that IBM was back, big time, and that a smart and gutsy leader was driving the turnaround.

As Lou engaged in the zero-base, blank-page thinking that is such a vital component of this crash course, he found a powerful epiphany. He would link to the company's historic culture as a sales-driven business. In the dark period before Gerstner once again tied earnings to performance, you could rise through the ranks at IBM by breathing. From now on, you had to sell your way up the ladder. No mission statements. No PowerPoints. No politics. To succeed in Lou's world, you had to contribute to the growth of the business. Raises gave way to commissions and bonuses. Everything was measurable. Nothing was guaranteed. A bloated bureaucracy turned into a free-market meritocracy.

As Gerstner proved to IBMers, customers, Wall Street, and the media, he was all about taking control . . . taking names . . . taking command . . . And he wasn't afraid to declare war on himself (as he learned how to succeed in a new company and an alien industry) and on what had become Anemic Blue. What he accomplished at IBM—and what I'm imploring you to accomplish, whether you run a multinational computer behemoth or sell lamps in a retail store—was far from easy. Employee inertia, entrenched bureaucracy, and the tyranny of the mediocre assailed Gerstner at every turn. Similar pitfalls and obstacles will likely challenge you. How do you beat them?

Perhaps I can offer a solution in the context of a personal experience. Several years ago I took temporary managerial control of *Success* magazine, a financially distressed publication with a long and checkered history. My assignment was to stabilize the business until a new CEO could be brought on board. At the end of week one, I was set to attend a meeting with the circulation department. Things weren't going well on the subscription front, and I had to find out why. As I walked into a shopworn conference room in the company's fourth-floor offices, the conversation that had been going on suddenly fell silent.

I could smell an ambush in the works.

The circulation team painted a virtual bull's-eye on my back. Whoa, I could feel the poison-tipped arrows whizzing toward me. The new boss (me)—a publishing novice who didn't know squat about circulation—would get his comeuppance. They could smell blood. It was going to be that kind of meeting. Or so they thought.

Let me stop for a moment to explain what a circulation department does. To be honest, no one really knows. They are supposed to identify the algorithm that turns direct-response marketing programs into paid subscriptions. The problem is that direct response is one form of marketing that quickly reveals the imposters. You can't hide behind Pyrrhic victories such as "we increased mind share" or "we have grown brand awareness." Try taking that to the bank! Precisely because direct response is so transparent (as to who is winning and who is failing), the circulation gurus come to work, espouse endless mumbo jumbo about all kinds of statistics, and then provide advice that is so intentionally obtuse and complex that no one will challenge it for fear of appearing stupid. These are the self-protective rules of the Secret Society of Magazine Circulation Wonks.

Cut away all the camouflage, inbred jargon, and research tomes, and the bottom line is that they are supposed to drive up circulation in ways that prove profitable for the magazine. Hold that thought, because it becomes important to this story.

No sooner did the meeting begin than the wonks started tossing out their buzzwords, asking me what I thought about this, that, or some other quasi-scientific factoid, knowing full well I'd never heard of any of it before. I let this charade go on for about a half hour, and just as the gremlins were wallowing in the glow of their apparent victory ("This boss will be gone in a week"), I silenced the would-be lynch mob by firmly tapping my index finger on the conference table.

All eyes turned to me.

MS: I have to admit, I don't have a clue as to what you are talking about.

Reading their minds, I heard the wheels spinning ("The dumb bastard is going to be easier to knock off than we thought").

MS: But I have a question: Do you folks know what **you** are talking about?

("Whoa, what's this all about?")

MS: Folks, our circulation sucks. I mean, it sucks badly. Really big time. I'm truly embarrassed and you should be, too.

      But I guess you're not because no one here has voiced a word of concern. And yet you've all been on this once-proud magazine's payroll for years, even decades, and during that time—including these miserable slip-sliding years—circulation hasn't grown; it hasn't declined; no, it's fallen through the floorboards.

So this is the last meeting I am having with this team until my one-hundred-day plan for turning around the magazine is issued next week. Why? Because you have it all wrong. Dead wrong. I don't need to know anything about circulation right now other than it stinks. And I need to find a way to get it growing again. Soaring again. Leading our industry. I have to find that way because you guys haven't. So that's what I'll do. Until that time, consider yourselves on thin ice.

Meeting adjourned!

With that, I walked out of the room. Never looked back. I didn't have to. I knew that in my wake sat a band of deflated, shell-shocked circulation frauds. When my one-hundred-day plan was announced, a new circulation VP sat at the head of the table, empowered with my mandate to make her department the best in the industry. Joined by a few hand-picked business minds I trusted, we conducted our own Manhattan Project. We found a way to defeat the enemy—in this case, our competitors and the publication's legacy of incompetence in driving circulation. Our Manhattan Project led to a plan that we placed in the context of one hundred days because this creates expectation, drives resolve, and forces change. A deadline and a series of specific steps leading up to it impose discipline on a team. On our team. On your team. On you.

Before I move on, there's an important declare war tactic embedded in this story: *know when to walk out of a room. To say good-bye and leave.* If you endure countless meetings until the blood drains from your head, your people know they can strap you into a chair, control the agenda, and let dead issues drag on for weeks, months, years. When **you** believe the issue is settled—remember, you are a leader, not a follower, and you do not need to build consensus—walk out of the room without saying a word. Make it clear that under your watch, there will be no filibusters.

Talk about sending a message!

Your Manhattan Project is the equivalent of walking out of the room and returning with a battle strategy designed to lead the company where you want it to go.

The plan should accomplish the following:

- Identify a strategic objective.
- Make it clear that it must be achieved.

- Establish your role as the commander, who takes responsibility for the success of the project.
- Explain why the project is important to the company, its employees, its investors, and other stakeholders.
- Send a strong signal that your Manhattan Project is not open to debate. It will get done. On time. And with maximum impact. Nothing will stop you.

BEFORE YOU LAUNCH your Manhattan Project, ask yourself, "Where's the best place to start?" If you're facing a complex tangle of problems or riding a crest of success and want to manage the growth that goes with it, you might think that the most logical place to start effecting transformational change is at the *beginning*. But what is the beginning? Your instinct is to parachute into the source of the issue and initiate the process there. But that may be the *worst* thing you can do.

Starting at the *beginning* is often a telltale sign of management that sucks. Counterintuitive, I know, but *logic* and *good business* practice are not always the same. If they were, any logical and conventional thinker could be a brilliant warrior. It's never that easy. So often the paradoxical and iconoclastic thinker and doer is the one who vanquishes the straight-A-paint-by-numbers-magna-cum-laude *genius*.

A poor manager, faced with a challenge and determined to identify a nuclear solution, will start by forming a task force to investigate the issues. To her, that's the beginning of the Manhattan Project. The prudent place to start. Sensible and conservative.

And guaranteed to stall, postpone, or prevent decisive and innovative change.

Why?

Because starting at the *beginning* virtually guarantees that your change will be tentative, preliminary, and easy to sabotage by those in your organization who like things just the way they are. Who are nicely ensconced in their comfort thrones.

A leader has to initiate change by making a bold statement anywhere along the continuum and following it up with scene-stealing action. I had a conversation recently with an old friend, a gifted surgeon, that wonderfully brings to life the point about picking the place to make your stand. My friend specializes in the most difficult cases of cancer of the neck and head. He's been saving lives for over twenty-five years. During a walk in the woods, I asked him what makes a great surgeon. He pondered the question, trudged silently through the woods for a few moments, and then it hit him.

A good surgeon realizes that you don't always have to start an operation at the beginning. Sure, the medical texts might tell you to, but as you mature in your practice, you learn to instinctively look backward and forward at the operating field . . . and to start where you think your skills can be best applied at that precise moment. For that given patient. If I always started where my professors at Harvard Medical School told me to start, I'd have lost patients that had no reason to die. Particularly in grave situations, you step up to the field and attack the problem not in linear fashion, but where your mind and heart and experience and guts indicate you can make the biggest impact.

If you want to join the ranks of the warriors, you'll need to engage in a similar assessment and the action that flows from it. When my friend faces a patient hemorrhaging blood on the operating table, he doesn't start by taking vital signs. Instead, he stops the bleeding and then backtracks to the causes of the bleeding. Similarly, if you're faced with the fact that your company or business unit is in need of dramatic action to manage growth, seize a major opportunity, or engineer a turnaround, don't establish a task force that will take three months to report back to you. Move to the vanguard of the issue and act there, creatively and decisively. Even if it is more of a scene-stealer (that changes perception) than a significant structural change.

Case in point: Whether you love or hate George W. Bush's politics, you have to admit that his surprise Thanksgiving appearance with the U.S. troops in Iraq was a stroke of genius.

The president's trip didn't change a thing about the reality of the war. Our soldiers were still fighting . . . people on both sides were still dying . . . Iraq was not one iota more secure after Bush's visit.

And yet, Bush's trip changed *everything*—even if only temporarily—about the perception of the Iraqi situation. It made the statement that Iraq was no longer under Saddam's control. That the president of the United States could come and go in that country as he pleased. That Iraq was *free*—in a symbolic, if not a literal, sense.

In short, the Iraqi visit had great marquee value. It made a high-profile statement that Bush—and the United States— was serious about changing the status quo. (Bush failed to declare war on himself and in turn on his Iraq strategy, and that hurt him in the end, but if he had decided to make a sea change in his approach, the surprise visit would have been the ideal way to send a signal.) The idea is to take the offensive. Prompt your people to say, "Whoa, he is serious about this."

Every person who worked on Roosevelt's Manhattan Project understood, in spades, that the president was determined to vanquish the enemy, not to be fair or open or humane—but to win. By forming and empowering the Manhattan Project, he was demonstrating leadership at a time and in a scenario where winning would take an extraordinary effort. You will face that in your career. Recognizing the importance of launching a Manhattan Project—and how to execute it with precision and resolve—will prove to be invaluable.

When launching your Manhattan Project as a warrior manager, regardless of your level in the organization you must:

- Identify problems and opportunities for what they are. (Resist the urge to sugarcoat anything.)
- Attack them at the point that promises to have the greatest impact. (Reject the start-at-the-beginning nonsense.)
- Choose to make changes that deliver the most impact. (Stop the bleeding, get the airwaves open, then move on to the longer-term fixes.)

As you plan your Manhattan Project, go out of the office. Be alone or with a trusted adviser. Close the door and think. Ask yourself, what's right? What's wrong? What excites you? What frightens you? Free-associate. Draw pictures. Use cartoon imagination. Take out your magic wand.

Some years ago, I asked the head of an entrepreneurial business unit at one of the nation's oldest manufacturers what she would do if she had a magic wand and could use it to effect change. At the time, she was locked in a wrestling match with other members of the management team. She asked for forty-eight hours to think about it—and then we met.

BELINDA: My problem—if we can call it that—belongs in the theater of the absurd. You know that my team is responsible for selling our oldest product, the one everyone else here gave up for dead. We recognized it didn't die a natural death. It was murdered by everyone who thought it was a relic of the past. That its time had come and gone. But we recognized it was still a good product in need of a powerful dose of marketing, and we injected it with dollars and passion and a sex appeal based on a retro concept. And it soared. And now I manage the hottest business unit in the company. And everyone wants my hide because they think I make them look bad.

But to hell with that: I am determined to grow this business even faster. As I took my team through our Manhattan Project, my thinking evolved. At first, I wanted to start slamming the most contentious departmental VPs, the ones who seem to get no greater joy than blocking every idea I have, every action I take. I wanted to confront them, find the skeletons in their closets, broadcast their failures, and reveal them for the enemies of progress that they are. I wanted the entire organization to know that they are frauds and backstabbers and gremlins that are holding the company hostage. I wanted to see them being led out of the office in handcuffs, with Eliot Spitzer reading them their rights. Oh, I was mad!

But I realized that in spite of the psychic rewards that would provide, the turmoil it would cause would make it harder to get through the execution phase of my project. I could see the jungle of politics and backlash tangling all around me.

So, I decided to use my magic wand more productively: I would take the CEO and COO out to lunch, show them the strategy I'd developed, and have them initiate a policy that would give me the runway to achieve my goals without interference from the political linebackers and without having to spend my time dealing with the carnage my first instinct would produce.

Launching your Manhattan Project is serious business. Like the mother of all projects for which it is named, there are huge risks associated with it. You are putting a stake in the ground. You are declaring that you will accomplish major initiatives. Will you deliver, or will this be a false promise? Will you prove yourself to be a warrior manager or a paper tiger? It's all on the line here.

The biggest blunder you can make is to fail to follow through on your Manhattan Projects. To take the inevitable heat and keep moving upstream. To accept failure. But time after time, Manhattan Projects are launched with enormous fanfare, cannons blasting, trumpets blaring—and are then allowed to fizzle out. Go south. Become flavor-of-the-month programs that pass from the scene with the impact of a tropical sun shower.

How does this happen? The question drives to the heart of management that sucks. More than any other asset, great managers have credibility. No one wonders if they are serious about what they say. When Bill Gates declared that he will pursue a search engine to compete with Google, no one thought he was playing parlor games. When Sandy Weill declared that he is going to reorganize Citigroup and fire his heir apparent/ golden boy/second in command, no one thought he was going to get talked out of it or buckle under pressure from the board. And yet time after time, managers/business owners/CEOs/ department heads—leaders at every stage of their careers and every-size companies and business units—allow their Manhattan Projects to become corporate jokes, stalled someplace between the fanfare and the finish line.

Understanding why these initiatives short-circuit can help you to prevent the same failures from undermining your power/credentials/credibility/career. The most common land mines:

- The "Bad Day" strikes and the manager runs for cover. There's no way you are going to announce a Manhattan Project and people aren't going to go bananas. Their jobs will be at risk. Their budgets are in jeopardy. They'll have to work harder and smarter. Many will resist. They'll bitch and moan.

Go behind your back to a superior. Leak news to the media. The question is, will you be strong enough to tough it out? Just when you are in the thick of it, think of the tidal wave Ronald Reagan had to endure when he fired the air-traffic controllers. *Fired the air-traffic controllers!* Buckling on that single issue would have jeopardized his entire presidency. He didn't. And you can't. So be sure you have the nerve to see it through before you think or say the words "My Manhattan Project."

● Minutia distracts the manager. You know the drill. You want to accomplish something big/something major/ something Super Bowl and then the tactical stuff comes flying at you.

E-mails/phone calls/meetings/sudden emergencies/ unexpected opportunities/customers drop in/your spouse has a problem/your kid wants to switch colleges. Precisely because you are a driven person who honors all of your responsibilities, you field these duties and keep pushing the Manhattan Project to the back burner.

Categorize this as a mistake. A sure way to sabotage yourself. Yes, your other duties need to be addressed, but in the midst of the Manhattan Project, nothing is more important than moving that ball down the court. Every day, you have to make progress in honoring your commitment. If life gets in the way—and it always will—adhere to this basic principle:

Stay in the office later and get it done.

- Work at home on the weekends to make sure the big picture isn't suffering one iota from lack of attention.

- Have your assistant and family members pitch in on personal responsibilities they can cover while you are delivering on one of the most important initiatives of your career.

- Make sure your team doesn't let up.

Remember, the minutiae were there before you launched your monster program. And they will be there after it is under way. Find a way to downgrade the minutiae until you've accomplished what you promised yourself and your team you would do. In spades. (No one ever rises to the top or builds a great business unit simply by doing all the little stuff right. It's important, sure, but it's not the only stuff in the warrior's world.)

A Manhattan Project is not a gimmick. It is a demonstration of managerial strategy and resolve. If you are prepared to follow through, to stay on course, to endure a bad day, to force the issue, to take the heat, to lead, it can pay big dividends. And more than that. It can drive fundamental change in your business unit, establish you as a warrior manager, dramatically enhance and upgrade your stature in the company, demonstrate that you are greater than the sum of your parts, and provide you with the hero stripes that prompt your team to want to follow you. Wherever you lead. No matter how challenging the assignment.

That's POWER.

Capturing Ideas with a Butterfly Net

Sometimes I think of myself as a man in a field, armed with a butterfly net. Capturing ideas.

It's the best job in the world. Day after day, I walk smack into the middle of the greatest stories in the world. Stories of people and the businesses they manage. The careers they build, destroy, and seek to rebuild. The fortunes they dream of, make, and squander. The politics that swirl around them. The smarts and nerve and verve and fear and drive and determination and passion they bring to capitalism. To their family-owned furniture chain. To their Fortune 500 global enterprise. To their first jobs. To what they hope won't be their last.

In each scenario, I am in the thick of it, gloves off, sleeves rolled up, working side by side to help them succeed. I'm not there as an observer; I'm there to help shape the agenda, develop the strategy, pick up the pieces, declare war, declare peace, open new markets, introduce products, mentor juniors, and advise leaders. Nothing could be more intoxicating. Each day I go in smart and come out smarter.

Why?

Because of those beautiful, elusive, compelling, and invaluable *ideas.*

Managing is a process of continuous discovery. Those

who rise from the pack, grow, expand, and become even more knowledgeable and experienced leaders do so in great measure because they absorb what they learn and employ it in the iterative process of personal growth. They know instinctively that continuous learning and the application of that knowledge drives them to the improved version of themselves that lies out before them as a target and a goal.

Let me share with you a number of powerful ideas I have *captured* in the course of my work. Ideas you can reflect on, nuance, personalize, and incorporate into your management style or store in the back of your brain for use when the time is right.

IDEA ❶ Almost every business overlooks its biggest cost: the opportunity it forfeits to generate incremental revenue due to a limited or myopic view of the world.

Let's look at it this way: Companies like to view the costs of doing business in pie-chart form, with each slice of the pie representing a category of costs.

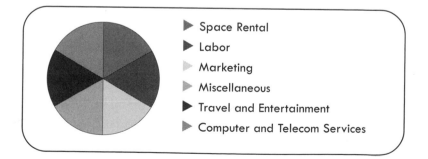

▶ Space Rental
▶ Labor
▶ Marketing
▶ Miscellaneous
▶ Travel and Entertainment
▶ Computer and Telecom Services

But the more accurate accounting (from the standpoint of leveraging business opportunity) is to consolidate all traditional costs into a single wedge of the pie and allot the balance of the pie to the biggest (but generally ignored) cost: OPPORTUNITY.

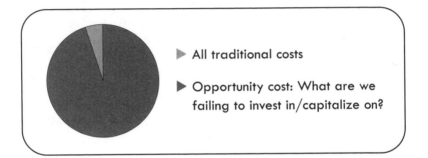

▶ All traditional costs

▶ Opportunity cost: What are we failing to invest in/capitalize on?

The point is that while you are focused on the costs of doing business (as you should be), the costs of failing to do business to your maximum potential takes a greater toll on your business unit's finances—and in turn, on your management performance. Think of it this way: Over time, every company, every business unit, every department winds up flying with blinders on. That's because management fails to ask:

- Who else can we sell to?
- Which new markets can we penetrate?
- How can we cross-sell more effectively?
- Do we have the flexibility to increase our prices?

All are opportunities the company may fail to explore. The revised cost pie chart makes it clear that the focus on traditional and tangible costs is myopic and surprisingly damaging to the fate of the enterprise. That's because it fixates on the expense side of the ledger while paying minimal attention to the revenue side. And that's where the growth arises. With this in mind, you will want to explore every opportunity to widen your business model without jeopardizing your current positioning and value proposition in the marketplace. In addition to asking yourself what it costs to pay for business expenses, you have to ask yourself what it costs to ignore or overlook opportunities.

When you achieve this difficult but highly achievable goal, the company grows, often exponentially, creating an enormous wellspring of sales and profits that can be leveraged with modest capital investments. The lesson here is to create the new pie chart, hang it on your wall, pass it out to your employees, and incorporate the relentless drive toward opportunity into your management agenda.

IDEA ❷ Now and then it hits you that you're doing the job of everyone who reports to you. This (a) demoralizes your direct reports, who come to think that you'll second-guess their every decision, (b) distracts you from making the big decisions that can establish or maintain your posture as a leader, and (c), most important, limits your time to explore and cultivate new opportunities.

The goal is to avoid the Land of the Inverted Work Model, where the bosses work and the employees observe.

Case in point: Lucy—a senior sales executive with a $200 million software company—was suffering from classic symptoms of management that sucks.

- She was unwilling to risk being unpopular, for fear this would jeopardize her ability to inspire people.
- Related to this, she was an "I need everybody to love me" consensus builder.

This highly intelligent woman fervently believed that the way to demonstrate her value to the company was to do the jobs of the people who reported to her. Conversely, that stripped her of the time, energy, stature, and credibility to grow the business.

Let's take a closer look at this. Lucy's business unit has six regional heads of sales, each leading teams of salespeople, including top producers. If you've ever spent time managing salespeople, no one has to tell you that they are always bitching about something—that's the nature of the breed. And paradoxically, the more successful they are and the more money they make, the more they complain. And the more empowered they feel to go over their boss's head and take their gripes right to the head of sales or directly to the CEO.

This makes managing a sales force difficult. Sure, your frontline sales people are essential, especially the top producers, but you cannot allow them to end-run their managers and come to you. If you do, they've taken your managers' jobs, and prevented them from doing theirs. And you've clogged your calendar with so much handholding, dispute settling, and babysitting, there's no way you can cultivate new opportunities (the lifeblood of every business).

In Lucy's case, any time her sales heavy hitters were unhappy—about a commission rate, a credit opinion, or whatever—they would petition her to reverse the decisions her direct reports, the regional sales managers, made and support their position. Which she did time and again (need to be loved . . . need to be loved). In falling victim to this trap, Lucy was stripping away the power of her sales managers and allowing herself to sink into the granular stuff, where followers, not leaders, thrive.

Lucy was wallowing in monster dysfunctionality. My job was to challenge her self-defeating behavior not with motivational gobbledygook, but with compelling facts—projected in graphic format—that would help her see not only the error of her ways, but also, equally important, the powerful elegance the truth revealed.

For this, I decided to show Lucy the opportunity-cost pie

chart (which served in this case as a metaphor for focusing on the wrong things and allowing the big opportunities to sail by). Instantly, she understood the real cost of the Inverted Work Model. She recognized that her drive to do the work of others, and in turn to be loved, was depriving her business unit of its growth potential because it distracted her from her true managerial role: to identify and cultivate growth opportunities. Every day she spent on handholding and caretaking and sweeping up after others, she was failing to drive the business forward. This graphic view of her myopia prompted her to break a bad habit and to turn the Inverted Work Model on its head.

On stage at the company's national sales meeting, Lucy declared war, establishing the new order of things:

- She would no longer respond to specific issues raised by members of the sales team.
- She distributed a list of responsibilities she now deemed to be the exclusive domain of her sales managers.
- She made it clear that taking these issues directly to her would be considered a violation of the rules.

Lucy then set out her personal business agenda, demonstrating that she would focus on the primary role senior management had entrusted to her, and that would propel her team's collective growth and—as she now recognized—her career trajectory: the identification and pursuit of strategic initiatives that would provide the company with exponential improvement in its sales methodologies and the cultivation of breakthrough opportunities.

Lucy was now free of the shackles she had imposed upon herself. In her world, the Inverted Work Model was history.

IDEA ❸ Conventional wisdom holds that every business's first priority is to serve its customers. I say no to that. You must treat them as members of an exclusive club.

How can I challenge the need to serve customers? And why am I so adamant about it? Because *serving* customers is incomplete and leads to a distorted and ineffective business model. What you really have to do is far more challenging and exponentially more rewarding. You have to build a 360-degree Customer Experience. In doing so, your business will revolve around your customers. So much so that they are no longer *customers*. They are *members* and *guests* of the company.

The 360-Degree Customer Experience

Building your business around members and guests—instead of the standard transactional view of serving customers—means that you and your team will:

Anticipate their needs	vs.	Respond to their needs
Exceed their expectations	vs.	Meet their expectations
Thrill them	vs.	Satisfy them
Surprise them with gestures of thoughtfulness	vs.	Give them everything they expect
Wrap them in a cocoon of products and care	vs.	Give them access to services
Make certain they fall in love with your company	vs.	Be satisfied if they like you
Offer them a lifetime of unique experiences and values	vs.	Close a sale
Commit to them	vs.	Be willing to take their next order

Here's why this 360-degree customer experience is so important: I attend dozens of client meetings a year, and we talk about everything under the sun—HR, productivity, cash flow, operations, competition—but hardly ever is the word "customer" uttered from anyone's lips. It's as if the companies operate without customers. As if their revenue is derived through divine intervention. Many companies get so absorbed with an internal view of the world that their customers' needs are filtered out of the strategy.

Case in point: Self-storage facilities dot the map from

coast to coast; operations and finance guys built and run these facilities and, typically, they don't have the customer on their radar screens. So they built a system that historically has treated customers with benign neglect. When business-people come into the storage facilities to check on their merchandise and throw out what they no longer need, they run into a problem captured in the words "throw out." How? Some of the companies don't have a single trash can at their storage centers. From the operations guys' perspective, they would have to clean the trash cans and maintain them, and why bother. The customer wants them, but in the world of operations execs, the customer doesn't count. The 360-Degree Customer Experience challenges this sad state of affairs and changes the way the companies interface with customers, who need to be perceived as the businesses' most valuable assets.

The 360-Degree Customer Experience is proactive, perpetual, protective, and personal. There is a continuum at work here. Think of the customer as a person/family first experiencing your business. The 360-Degree Experience is designed to transition the customer into a member of your *family* by showering him or her with all of the unique components, resources, and services of your business. And then to move onward from there, building a lifelong relationship with the *family member.*

This frontline strategy is built on the proven (ask Wal-Mart) principle *that extraordinary experience and startling service wins customers for life.*

IDEA ④ Great managers never fall in love with ideas and then act. First they measure the upside and worst-case scenarios. Why? Because they know that behind every dream scenario lies a flophouse in Reno.

Have you ever been to Reno, Nevada? If you've had the *pleasure,* you know it's a postage stamp of a place cluttered with ugly buildings and garish casinos.

On a recent visit, it struck me that amid the neon fireworks of the gaming icons flashing such names as Harrah's and Golden Nugget across the skyline, drab little hotels stand like stepchildren in virtual obscurity.

Who would stay at these virtual flophouses? I wondered. They don't have gambling. They're not exactly vacation spots. How and why do they survive here? Precisely the question I asked Rhonda, a local business associate, as she was driving me through town on our way to a plastics-industry luncheon. (Funny how American industry loves to hold its off-sites in the sleaze capitals of the nation.) By the bemused look on her face, I could tell Rhonda had been asked that question a thousand times before. "Not a pretty story," she said. "They don't write about this one in the tourist guides."

And then she launched into the tawdry details.

RHONDA: Behind the business conventions and the gambling junkets, there's a subculture of bet-the-farm folks who clean out their bank accounts, extract the equity from their homes, buy a plane ticket, and come to Reno to put their life's work on the line.

Something creeps into their heads that they are on the verge of the Big Strike. Sinatra is singing "Luck Be a Lady." The time is now. That place is Reno. The planets are aligned.

In a day—sometimes within hours—the Big Strike morphs into the Big Bust. They're on the streets: broke, rejected, deer-in-the-headlights lost souls. The only thing they can do is book a room in these joints and try to figure out how and if they will go on with their lives.

Now, I don't think anyone reading this book is on the verge of booking a bet-the-farm junket to Reno. But as a businessperson, you don't have to leave your office to take risks. Your office is the risk capital of the world. The epicenter. It is where you make decisions to spend budgets, start ventures, invest money, find partners, acquire a competitor, go public, and develop strategies.

So many of the moves you make and fail to make (remember the demon of opportunity cost) involve risk. Risk to your performance, reputation, compensation, position, and career. The axiom "The greater the risk you are willing to take, the higher the returns you can reap" is often true, but that doesn't mean you should throw caution to the wind. Finding the delicate balance between the willingness to accept risk and maintaining a deep respect for business discipline will serve you well. This is especially true as you declare (constructive) war on yourself, your business unit, your bad habits, and your personal MO. As you ponder this balance and seek to achieve it, another axiom should factor into your thinking: "If you can't do the time, then don't do the crime."

So let's follow the bouncing ball. Where should you draw the line in deciding on your personal risk tolerance? How do you navigate successfully in the shark-infested gray area that lies between "I'd like to take that risk, but I'm not sure I can accept the consequences if I bet wrong."

One of the themes of this book is simplicity, and here again simplicity rules. *Never take a risk that should you lose; you'll end up (metaphorically) in a flophouse in Reno.*

When I contemplate a risk, I always picture the worst-case scenario of accepting it or rejecting it. If either decision led to a major loss, could I brush myself off and start again? Or would I feel there would be little chance for recovery?

As you analyze risk, consider the importance of developing and employing a personal philosophy. Remember my brief portrait of financier and takeover artist Carl Icahn. Throughout his extraordinary career, he has demonstrated the importance of basing business decisions not on emotions or even pure financial calculations. People who underestimate Icahn, who negotiate with him and lose, who threaten him and then wind up filling his bank account with treasure, think of him as a financial guy. But Carl is far more than that.

He is a businessman-philosopher. He has demonstrated the value, the power, of basing decisions on philosophy.

As *you* face and address risk, you will want to avoid the all-too-common approach of making decisions in a vacuum, without the benefit of a personal philosophy. A philosophy that will help you decide under what circumstances you will accept significant risk and where you will draw the line against it. As you do so, recognize that there is no right or wrong—only a personal approach to decision making that is consistent with your strengths, your values, your DNA.

Personally, I can never do anything that if it failed, would dead-end me in a flophouse in Reno. I faced this ugly possibility when four dot-com clients imploded in 2001, leaving MSCO with millions of dollars of media bills we had signed for on the clients' behalf. I was concerned about my company's financial well-being . . . and ultimately my family's. Every option for dealing with the crisis crossed my mind. In the end, it boiled down to two: (1) bankrupt the business, leave the creditors high and dry, and start a new company; or (2) pay off the debt and learn a lesson (about accepting clients' financial obligations) from the torment I would endure.

Selecting option two, I authorized my controller to negotiate with vendors and start paying the bills under the best terms we could get. Compounding this mess, even as we were owning up to the problem, new bills from printers and other vendors were appearing with disturbing regularity. The business was becoming a money pit: The more we paid, it seemed, the more we owed. Granted, I had a financial controls issue to deal with, but that didn't change the fact that MSCO owed a ton of money and we couldn't see the light at the end of the tunnel.

Stuck in this quicksand, a new question arose: How far would I go to honor clients' debts? To save my business? My original decision—painful but at the time appropriate—was that I would pay off all of the debt, clear the decks, and be a wiser businessperson going forward.

But what were my limits if these debts kept piling up? I knew I could endure a payback of up to $5 million.

But what if debt soared to $10 million? Or $20 million? Or more? This is where my "don't bet the farm" philosophy kicked in. Extracting my emotions, I did a financial calculation, engaged in a philosophical gut check about the flophouse in Reno, and then drew a line in the sand. I would pay up to a certain amount and no more! If the bills continued to mount, putting my personal finances in jeopardy (because I was funding some of the debt with my own money), I would fold the company and walk away.

I came uncomfortably close to the brink. And then the world turned. The sun came out. No new bills showed their ugly heads. Yes, I had lost millions of dollars of personal wealth. Yes, my company's cash position was weakened. But MSCO's methodology was still strong. We had honored clients' obligations. We stayed in the arena and fought. We served an illustrious group of clients. We had tomorrow on our side, and we would make it the best time in the company's history. Which we have done. In spades. My philosophy for managing risk gave me a window to move through a period of adversity and provided a safety net against the nightmare of waking up in a flophouse in Reno.

It's time to look at your philosophy for managing risk.

IDEA ⑤ Know when to take a "clown vote" and have the guts to cast the only ballot (think of it as using your power, unilaterally, when those around you prefer to filibuster).

The day before 9/11 changed the world (just an eerie coincidence), my office received a call from the CEO (we'll call him Henry) of a relatively obscure (for a business with $3 billion in annual sales) NASDAQ-listed company, asking us to help them wrestle into submission an issue they'd been struggling with for years. When my executive vice president passed the call to me, Henry was on the line.

HENRY: We've never proactively explored markets outside of North America. Yet we know we have major opportunities across the globe, particularly in Europe and Latin America, where research demonstrates tremendous demand for our products. Our suppliers and other partners tell us this is a virtual slam dunk. That we could claim big chunks of market share virtually overnight.

As Henry is waxing poetic, I'm thinking, "If something sounds too good to be true, it probably isn't true. There's likely a missing puzzle piece."

MS: Henry, respectfully, if the markets are aching for your products—and at this point I have no reason to doubt your research—why do you need me and MSCO? You know how to sell in North America; why not simply train your sales and marketing guns abroad? Are you worried about navigating through the markets' cultural differences?

HENRY: Well, no. Not really. How can I say this? The issue is more internal than external. For this reason, our biggest opportunity—leveraging overseas markets— is also our biggest challenge. More than a challenge. It's a goddam migraine!

              That's why we need you and your people.

MS: I'd love to see if we could help. Can you tell me more, Henry?

HENRY: A sizable contingent of our team thinks we should be content to grow in the markets we know and avoid the risks of reckless expansion.

That was all Henry had to say. Experience told me "reckless expansion" was corporate code for "Let's stay in our comfort thrones, collect our paychecks, and let other companies take the risks of global ambition. We have a good thing going—why mess with it?"

If this was the scenario, I'd seen it a thousand times before. It had all the markings of a shortsighted, obstructionist group failing to recognize that no business can simply stay in place. Economics, consumer trends, competition—all will infringe on the cocoon of riskless growth. Every business must conscientiously move out of its comfort zone or it will inevitably fall behind.

Ten days later (with the airports virtually deserted in the aftermath of 9/11), three members of the MSCO team and I were on a United Air Lines flight bound for Denver. We arrived at the company's offices and were ushered up to the thirty-second-floor boardroom (adorned, ironically, by a photo montage of breathtaking global vistas). Quickly, my attention turned to the twelve senior managers in the room— all men, all dressed in black suits and white shirts—carefully positioned around the long marble conference table, surrounding the MSCO contingent. (If the language I'm using sounds a bit ominous, you'll understand why in a moment.)

As soon as I walked through the door I knew I was in for a tough time. The silence in the conference room was deafening. No one from Henry's team said hello to us. No break-the-ice chitchat. Not even a superficial welcome. Everyone but Henry (who managed a forced smile) was grim, tight-lipped, and silent.

The "home team"—Henry, his CEO, Connor, and their band of ten—were seated at the far end of the conference table. My team and I were seated so far away it felt like another zip code.

I thought I'd break the ice.

MS: First time I've been to a star chamber. We plead innocent.

No one cracked a smile.

As we moved into our hot seats, Henry took the floor, laying out the reason MSCO was invited to an audience with the princes of the company. He introduced MSCO, focusing on my credentials as a corporate adviser who had aided an illustrious list of companies and would be the ideal person to guide all in attendance through their global challenge. With that flourish, Henry came to a hard stop, allowing the room to go silent. Clearly, it was my turn to live up to that introduction, impressing a group that had no desire to be impressed by anyone or, for that matter, to change its business practices one iota.

I began by trying to introduce my team. But within seconds of my opening remarks, the missiles were launched.

- "Who are you?"
- "What do you know?"

- "Why the hell are you here?"
- "What are you selling?"

It was Kafkaesque. I was in court, subject to cross-examination, without knowledge of what I was accused. And the verbal barrage went from bad to vitriolic.

- "Why venture into untested waters when we virtually mint money in North America?"
- "Advisers like you force companies to assume reckless risk."
- "You can't guarantee we'll succeed in new markets!"
- "We really don't need anyone telling us how to run our business."

The assault continued for nearly four hours. FOUR HOURS! The MSCO team members by my side—experienced, outspoken, strong, extroverted, and intelligent executives—had completely shut down after the first hour. None had ever experienced anything like this baptism by fire. Like this would-be lynch mob.

I found myself on my own, duking it out with closed-minded suits and Henry, who was now questioning his own judgment in seeking to serve as a catalyst for change.

Part of me said, "This is futile. Collect your initial consultation fee and beat it."

But another voice rose to the top: "Screw these guys. Tell them exactly what they don't want to hear."

Turning the tables, seizing the agenda, I lambasted them, charging that they were mired in complacency, self-indulgence, fear of change, and management by autopilot. And I went on to assert that unless they declared war on their own business practices, they would be seriously jeopardizing the future of their business.

Just as I thought I was in the zone, that my impassioned pushback had broken through the wall of resistance, one of the boys in the band rose from his seat and proceeded to point his right index finger at me.

"You're making the assumption that we should sell our products in Europe and Latin America, but we haven't come to that conclusion yet. Not by a long shot. We study things in this company. Perhaps the other companies you work with take rash measures, but we haven't become as successful as we are by acting on capricious whims."

I was dumbstruck . . . and incensed.

MS: Excuse me, but have I been dreaming? Didn't I hear Henry say that you've been studying this opportunity for four years? We won World War II in less time. You have markets that are eager to have your products. Your own research—backed by your agents on the ground—raises only one question:

What the hell are you waiting for? Rash? Whims? Gentlemen, this is anything but that. We're talking about good, sound business judgment.

Just as the forces were about to counterattack, Connor, the CEO, awoke from a self-imposed silence. Raising his right hand in the air, he declared, "Let's take a vote."

He hadn't said a word the entire meeting, and now he wants to take a vote. What kind of leader is this? A real leader wouldn't need or want to take a vote at this point. And then a moment later, Connor went down in my book of managerial marvels. Of heroes. Of men and women who are greater than the sum of their parts.

Walking along the circumference of the conference table, his hand still raised to prompt the vote, Connor asked his lieutenants, "Which one of you fucking clowns thinks we shouldn't expand globally as Stevens is advocating? I repeat, which one of you fucking clowns thinks we shouldn't take Stevens's advice?"

Ta-da! Sun pierced through the drawn blinds and lit the conference room. It was near biblical. All of the suits did a 180:

- "Oh yeah, definitely we should do this."
- "Totally agree. And MSCO is the company to take us into those new markets."
- "Clearly, the time has come to act."

Long story short: Connor launched his company on a global expansion that has scored bull's-eyes in Japan, India, China, and Latin America and is now bearing down on eastern Europe. Less than three years later, more than 25 percent of the company's profits are now generated outside of North America.

Connor demonstrated the rare managerial gift of knowing how and when to apply power. Determined not to be a micromanager, Connor had always allowed his managers to function with a great deal of autonomy.

He believes that warriors don't manage their business units; they drive them to achieve exceptional growth. Reluctant to meddle in the day-to-day minutiae, he accepts the internal tug of war as independent-minded managers create and defend their own agendas. But when he recognizes that his subordinates cannot get past their internal bickering, he acts decisively and with a perfect sense of timing and theater.

I've known far too many managers who do not know when to order a *clown vote,* and sooner or later this takes a punishing toll on the business units they are charged to run (and that wind up running them).

How and when to use your power most effectively:

- When people least expect it . . . as in Connor's surprise attack. (I think of this as being asymmetrical.)

- When you believe that the failure to exert your power will allow the company to squander opportunities.

- When a vacuum will be created if the *leader* fails to lead.

- When you can make a statement that will "silence the room" based on its insight/integrity/wisdom/truth. And that *silence* will prove to be a powerful learning experience and a catalyst for change.

IDEA ⑥ Your greatest skill is a double-edged sword: it empowers and limits your company simultaneously.

Gene runs a consulting business specializing in the development of new versions of standard life-insurance products: term, whole life, and variable life. Most of the life-insurance industry is stuck selling one basic promise: We'll provide your heirs with a lump sum of cash when you die. Because MetLife and Prudential and the Hartford and the legion of companies in this highly competitive industry have to make the same promise, they need ways to distinguish their products over their competitors'. So the industry is continuously developing variations on a theme in the form of new twists on venerable life-insurance products designed to reduce the premiums, provide greater cash values, allocate premium dollars to equity investments, extend the coverage periods, and on and on and on. This flavor-of-the-month marketing is how the sales folks—who are at the heart of the companies' revenue-producing machines—win new customers (often by telling them that the policy they now hold is a Model T). So if it's some new breed of life-insurance product the companies want to create and sell, Gene's their man.

Gene is a rocket scientist: He's got this great mathematical/analytical/financial mind for creating products that are financially sound for the buyer and highly profitable for the insurer.

After about a dozen years in the business, Gene looked around and was forced to admit that he was extraordinarily good at building life-insurance products and mediocre in the art and science of business building. With fifteen employees and annual revenues of less than $3 million, Gene had a long way to go to build a significant enterprise. What he had was a Gene machine. He could sell Gene's brainpower all day long, but he couldn't leverage that into a company that recruited and marketed other Genes or that created insurance-development software or that did anything at all to use Gene's unique position in a wealthy industry to build a $10 million, $20 million, or $50+ million business. One less dependent on Gene. Like so many entrepreneurs who are good at one thing or another, Gene based his business on a unique skill set: the ability to identify sales opportunities for new life-insurance products and to develop the mathematical calculations on which they would be based. Only Gene could deliver that magic to the firm's clients.

Gene made good money. He was well respected. He liked his work. But he didn't have a business with internal combustion. He had what I call a golf-cart company: Take your foot off the pedal, and it stops. That's not a business. It's a guy with a lemonade stand. Guy gets a cold. Guy goes to bed. No lemonade today. No money. The other people in the business—whose job is to grind what Gene mines—are administrative and secretarial staff that may do their jobs well but cannot generate revenue from new clients or through the organic growth of existing clients.

Graduating from a golf-cart company to a real business or department (one that can continue to run even when the manager takes his foot off the pedal) is a momentous transition. Every businessperson has to go through it. It takes the recognition that the best managers are dispensable. (God, the ego hates to hear that!)

Any business unit dependent on a single individual cannot grow to significant stature. It is boxed in. Dead-ended. A victim of its so-called leader. The greatest accomplishment I can achieve at MSCO is to leave the business for a year and know that it will do more than function effectively. That it will grow. That's the hallmark of a true manager. And, in turn, it's the difference between a growth machine and a Gene machine.

As Gene contemplated the growth of his firm, his initial thoughts focused on marketing. He would turn up the advertising and PR jets and presto, the company would soar. But he quickly recognized that the problem was not about getting his name on more radar screens. He enjoyed an enviable reputation in his industry, and new consulting engagements poured in spontaneously.

Gene's killer problem was that he sucked at management: great on the conceptual level, miserable at execution. Exhibiting entrepreneurial pigheadedness, he clung to the near-religious belief that he had to make all the decisions and do virtually everything himself. Instead of being the engine for growth, he was the brick wall: a walking, talking bottleneck that nearly paralyzed the business.

In classic fashion, Gene gloated over his failures:

On any given day, I must have twenty-five voice-mail messages backed up on my cell phone, waiting for me to respond. More than three-quarters of them are current clients who want to pick my brain, or hire us for new projects—and there's plenty more from prospects that have heard about us and want more information. Add to this stew the calls from employees who need guidance on client engagements, and, well, let's just say I don't get to everyone when I should. The world's waiting for me, and I have just so many hours in my day.

As hard as Gene worked, he never seemed to gain control of the business. The business controlled Gene. Leads, clients, projects, problems, opportunities, successes, and failures—all rolled in and out like the tides. Through it all, Gene lacked a philosophy and a process for prioritizing activities, setting goals, establishing performance standards, delegating responsibilities, capturing and converting leads, and proactively growing client relationships.

And Gene wondered why the golf cart came to a screeching halt whenever he took a day off.

GENE: I wish I could do things differently, more effectively. I know I am letting wonderful opportunities slip away because I don't respond to them in a timely manner. But no one else can handle the issues in this business while I tend to cultivating new opportunities. I'm just too important to the company.

The president of the United States is important, too—but he has a chief of staff to act as a gatekeeper and to delegate tasks. If the president didn't have such a person, he'd quickly become incapacitated by the minutiae of governing. As would every single person with the responsibility for managing people, budgets, initiatives, revenues, and profitability.

That's why every company and business unit needs to discover and implement a way to sustain itself—in fact, grow itself—without the manager sitting in the golf cart 24/7/365.

I advised Gene that he needed a chief of staff of his own, someone to handle all the details of the business, thus freeing Gene up for what he did best: developing innovative insurance products and networking with the top insurance executives in position to engage his company.

GENE: Yes, but the U.S. president's chief of staff is usually
        a close friend of the president. I don't have any
        friends who can help me. And I can't see myself try-
        ing to line up strangers to do the job.

Time to declare war. On a control freak. One who
couldn't contemplate trusting another individual with the
details of his business . . . even if it meant that person could
evolve into a valued lieutenant and collaborator capable of
rescuing Gene from the spider's web he'd fallen victim to.

Then, one night, Gene had me over to his house for dinner. "Jeans and strategy" is what I call these sessions. No
phone calls. No employee meetings. No interruptions of any
kind. Just good food, a glass of wine, and time to reflect and
strategize.

During the evening, it became clear to me that Gene's
wife, Nikki, was highly knowledgeable and perceptive about
the business: its financials, clients, and employees; and
Gene's competencies, Gene's weaknesses, and the threat
those weak points posed to the company and, in turn, the
couple's financial security. Nikki was outspoken, elegant,
strong-willed, and highly intelligent. A classic example of
what I call a sidelines manager—but in this case one with all
the right stuff to move out to the front lines.

Not only that, but she wasn't the least bit shy about
telling Gene what he needed to do to turn his golf cart into a
business. And so I pounced.

MS: Nikki, have you ever thought of working in the business?

Silence. And then:

NIKKI: I do have my family responsibilities and my charity work . . . but . . .

MS: Nikki, would you like to work in the business?

NIKKI: Well, I think . . . yes . . . actually, I would like it very much.

As Gene listened to the conversation, which proceeded well into the night, the look on his face went from threatened to uncertain to relieved that the answer to his problem might be his best friend in the world.

A month later, Nikki took the job. As I rethought the issues and challenges the company faced, and matched them with Nikki's skill set, it struck me that the business needed a chief operating officer and that Nikki was tailor-made for the job. I constructed a contract for both Gene and Nikki to review and sign, placing the terms in a legal framework. My goals were to:

- Achieve a high level of specificity.
- Avoid the informality of husband-and-wife collaboration. This would be all business.

As it has proven to be. Now in her fourth year and counting, Nikki is a superb COO, tying together what had been a collection of people operating under the same roof into an organization with structure, mission, specific duties, career paths, and collective goals. Most important, when Gene is busy creating new insurance products (his highest and best skills), the organization is still moving forward. Even when Gene's foot is a mile from the gas pedal. That's because Nikki and her team have it pressed to the metal.

If your company or department is a golf cart masquerading as a business, the time for change has arrived.

IDEA ⑦ Great salespeople don't just wind up at the same company . . . great managers lead them there, lavish them with rewards, and lock the door against imposters.

As soon as we meet, right at the beginning, I ask managers, "How's your sales organization?" I need to know how my client's sales force performs. Generates opportunities. Converts leads into customers. Stacks up well against the competition.

Invariably, my question elicits a knee-jerk but apparently assured response from the top honcho: "Our sales organization is really good. We've got a great sales team."

I want to believe them when they tell me this. I really do, like I want to believe in Santa Claus and the Tooth

Fairy. But I'm also a serial skeptic. I know from experience that a superb sales force is always the by-product of a strong sales culture and that these cultures don't materialize organically. They don't just happen. Someone who understands the power of sales drives the culture. They find great talent. They develop a methodology. They train on it. They treat salespeople like stars. They pay them handsomely when they perform. They give them trophies and dollars and applause and free vacations and champagne, and they carry them around the company meetings in sedan chairs.

A guy like Michael Dell recognized when he was a twenty-year-old student hawking desktops that if he was going to create a great enterprise, he would have to breathe sales into every crack and crevice of the company. It's hiring, training, promotions, compensation. He wasn't going to simply hire salespeople; he was going to bring them into a culture in which they could flourish.

Similarly, in its heyday, Xerox had one of the best sales organizations in the world. That didn't happen by accident. Xerox made it happen. How? By treating its salespeople like princes. If you were a star Xerox salesperson, you could fly first class wherever you went. That one gesture said volumes about the regard Xerox had for its sales team. Management understood how everything and everyone depended on the sale being made . . . and they carried the sales folks on their shoulders and fanned them on hot days.

Anyway, client management always says to me, "We've got a great sales team . . ."

Then I wait for the qualifier: "Of course, it's the old 80/20 rule. Twenty percent of our sales people generate 80 percent of our sales."

And I think to myself, "The 80/20 rule rides again."

You've probably heard this so-called *rule* a thousand ways:

- Twenty percent of your customers produce 80 percent of your revenues.
- Twenty percent of your employees do 80 percent of the work.

It goes on and on and on!

Most managers accept the 80/20 rule as gospel. The "insight" they glean from it is to heap special attention and incentive on that top 20 percent of the crop, because in one way or another they hold the fate of the business in their hands.

I choose to look at it another way: Whenever you are in the grips of an 80/20 scenario, something is rotten in Denmark.

- Eighty percent of your sales force sucks, and you're putting them in the field under the pretense that they can grow the business.
- Eighty percent of your employees suck, and you're still paying their salaries.

You're probably wondering, "What am I supposed to do? Just get rid of them?"

Absolutely. Remember, that's what I did with my employees in 2001. I didn't do it in a day. I didn't do it out of anger. I didn't do it without a plan. But I did it. I was determined to challenge the oxymoron of conventional wisdom: that we have to accept 80 percent of anything as subpar. Nonsense.

The 80/20 rule has been carved into tablets of the Ten Commandments of Business. Well, I say, "Smash the tablets."

Don't believe in the 80/20 rule. Instead, believe in the 100/100 rule:

- One hundred percent of your salespeople should able to close.
- One hundred percent of your customers should be well worth serving.
- One hundred percent of your employees should be working to grow the business.

Keep the best. And take out the rest. Declare war on mediocrity everyplace you see it. And be sure to look under the rocks: that's where it hides. Then fasten your seat belt. It will put your career into high orbit.

Applying C + A + M

The Universal Equation

for Perpetual Growth

As you prepare to complete this book and focus all that you have learned on your business unit, your career, and your life, I would like you to consider a powerful equation that can help you accomplish this. Think of it as a way of concentrating all of the elements of your war strategy into a simple, measurable, and manageable formula for achieving perpetual growth.

For generations, physicists have sought to develop the grand unifying theory (GUT), a paradigm for explaining all of the complex dynamics of the physical world in a concise and bulletproof framework. To date, they have failed. Newton's laws, Einstein's relativity, and string theory all break down around the edges. The work goes on, but the answer proves elusive.

Which led me to think: Is there a universal equation that can guide companies to achieve perpetual growth? My professional experience with people as diverse as Michael Bloomberg and former secretary of the treasury Bill Simon—and with a wide scope of companies moving through all phases of the business cycle—gives me evidence that the answer is yes. And you can find it in the pursuit of capturing customers, amplifying your relationships with them, and maintaining these relationships for life. Focus on these three critically important elements—capture, amplify, maintain—and you will achieve perpetual growth.

 hus the universal theory for growing your business unit:

$$C + A + M = PG$$

The beauty of our universal equation lies in its simplicity. Remember, a major thrust of this book revolves around simplifying the managerial/business building process. As you will see, all of the elements of business—human resources, corporate finance, manufacturing, customer service, internal operations—fold into one or more of the three CAM pillars. And because CAM is focused on the customer, you will see how to train these diverse functions and disciplines on the most important goal of your business: winning customers and making them deliriously happy. Viewing your world this way helps you to get to the essence. To simplify. To focus on the true levers of growth: $C + A + M$. Everything must be embedded in these essential drivers of growing businesses.

Case in point: Virginia is the proprietor of an offbeat women's clothing boutique in a funky San Francisco neighborhood undergoing gentrification. When asked what "keeps her up at night," she claims it's a deep-seated fear that her business isn't growing fast enough and may not make it as a going concern. Translation: Virginia fears that she is not capturing sufficient numbers of customers.

Her fear is well founded. Virginia believes she has the right merchandise at the right prices for her customer base, but all too often prospects leave the store without buying. She is failing to capture them.

Wait a minute. Virginia has the right merchandise well priced for the customer base and still suffers weak sales? What's missing from this picture? How about a puzzle piece the size of the Golden Gate Bridge. Virginia's story reminds me of the classic Hollywood admonition: "Make a bad movie and people will stay away in droves."

Virginia's bad movie is that she doesn't—contrary to her beliefs—have the right clothing at the right price. People don't walk out of stores without buying when the right merchandise is effectively stocked and priced. Why doesn't Virginia have the right goods in place? A misplaced focus on her personal tastes.

Check out this exchange.

MS: You say women come into your store and often leave empty-handed. Are there any items that they buy in significant quantities?

VIRGINIA: Well, I can't stock enough blue jeans. They just fly out of the store.

MS: Have you tried increasing the amount of floor space you allocate to jeans?

VIRGINIA: I don't want to do that.

MS: And why is that?

VIRGINIA: Because I have a personal distaste for jeans. I think everybody looks lousy in them. I don't think they're the right way to dress. I guess I'd rather sell nothing than sell jeans. I sell some, but I hate it.

MS: What you're really saying is that it is more important for you to be on a personal crusade against a particular type of fashion—in your case, jeans—than to capture customers for your business. Every time your customers scream at the top of their lungs, "Give us jeans, jeans, jeans!" you scream back at them, "That's bad taste. That's bad taste."

             Respectfully, Virginia, you say that wearing jeans as a fashion statement sucks, but what really sucks is the way that you are managing your business.

Clearly, Virginia is torn by a personal conflict between her opinion of proper personal appearance and her desire to behave as a successful businesswoman. She wakes up in the morning not sure what side of the bed to get out of—fashion crusader or retailer. Instead of putting her ear to the ground to identify and address her customers' desires, she turns a deaf ear to the request of the very people who can make her company a great success. To the people she must capture, build relationships with, and retain as valued customers—on their terms, not hers (or yours).

The focus on the universal equation of capturing, amplifying, and maintaining customer relationship is the blueprint for effective management. It is a living, breathing process that is at the center of your leadership. Whether you are managing one person or a massive organization, whether your enterprise is a restaurant, an IT department, or a global media empire, you must have a core strategy that drives your decisions.

As a manager, you face all of the following questions. Rather than dealing with them on a random basis, think about the $C + A + M = PG$ equation, identify where your business unit needs more firepower, and make the decision in this context.

- How and where do I allocate resources?

- How do I prioritize my tasks and those of my staff?

- On what basis are compensation, promotion, and bonuses granted?

- What skills do I need to attain and enhance to improve personal and collective performance?

With the focus on $C + A + M = PG$ embedded in your mind and your actions, all of your energy and assets are directed to the growth of the unit you manage. Extraneous issues such as corporate politics, vanity, grandstanding, and the pursuit of conventional wisdom are cast to the sidelines.

A simple example drives the issue home and demonstrates how the C + A + M equation directs the managerial process toward the universal goal of perpetual growth.

At some point in the year, you discover that you have $100,000 to reinvest in the unit you manage. Should you use it to redecorate your office, purchase a luxury car, add to a cash hoard, hire a salesperson, or build a customer-loyalty program? All of the above can be justified if you chose to justify them. But the last two—investing in a talented salesperson and creating or enhancing a customer-loyalty program—will do the most to support C + A + M. Thus, as a disciplined manager and leader, you have the basis for making your decision.

All of the components of C + A + M = PG must reinforce one another to achieve the synergies that lead to extraordinary growth. Let's begin by understanding the building blocks and see how they are organized under the umbrella of capturing, amplifying, and maintaining customer relationships.

Capture

The process of identifying prospects and converting them to customers is what capture is all about. To do so, you will need to create and develop an integrated set of sales and marketing tools and initiatives, all based around compelling messages, a powerful brand promise, and killer offers.

Let's view the capture phase in action. Microcomputer Consulting Group (MCG)—a twenty-year-old computer network management firm based in Manhattan—had achieved sound growth in a commodity market crowded with competitors all targeting the same prospects on the price-conscious, I-can-get-it-cheaper-from-someone-else isle of Manhattan. Still, the firm performed quality work and had built a loyal client base in a stable, slow-growth industry.

And then the opportunity to break out appeared. The potential meteor. The layup. CEO Ken Goldberg was introduced to a software product developed by X, one of the firm's business partners for the network-management side of the business. The company was exploring the idea of licensing the software to an exclusive group of resellers who would bring it to market through their own distribution channels. MCG liked what it saw and agreed to distribute the software.

The product enables computer users to place data in secure storage with a simple point-and-click technology. If you're working on an important document or spreadsheet and want it safe from loss, damage, or theft, the new product enables you to simply highlight the content, hit return, and bam—the precious digital cargo is whisked through cyberspace and sealed in a virtual vault at a remote location. It gives users peace of mind in a matter of seconds.

It is precisely the kind of simple and inexpensive solution that people adore, and also the kind that makes the entrepreneurs who bring it to market rich.

The product had big-time opportunity, and Ken and his partners at MCG set out to launch it in the New York area. They began to offer it to their existing customers as an extension of their traditional network-management services. The reaction was lukewarm. Prospects seemed to like what the product did, but not enough to buy it or to do so in sufficient quantities to make the software a success. The MCG management team had the guts to invest in something new but wasn't being rewarded for their entrepreneurial initiative.

At this point, Ken asked if I would consult with them. From the first meeting at MCG's offices, I recognized that the guys had to arrive at an important understanding.

MS: You are viewing this software as a new selling opportunity, but it is really more than that. By moving in this direction, you are transitioning from a service business to a product business. And there is a huge difference between the two. Furthermore, you don't know anything about marketing products, and you are going to have to get real good at it real fast if this is going to have a prayer.

KEN GOLDBERG: How would you suggest we start?

MS: By asking yourselves if you really have the stomach—and the capital—to segue from what you know how to sell (tech services) to what is a complete mystery to you (mass-market tech products).

BARRY X: I know that I speak for my partners when I say we do.

MS: Good. But let me warn you that it will be infinitely more challenging than you envision it to be—and, if you are successful, far more rewarding.

Although they were tech guys who barely thought about marketing throughout their careers, the MCG principals had taken the first stabs at marketing the software on their own. Everything they did was intelligent and workmanlike (such as introducing the product to their accounting-firm clients, viewing them as powerful referral sources), but none of it was about to set the world on fire—and great marketing has to shoot for that.

Problem number one was the software's name. MCG's management team had christened it Dupe Data. (I thought, "Did they have a contest and decide to hand the blue ribbon to the worst god-awful name they could create?") I mean, it sounded dopey and stupid and nothing that would help prospects understand what it does and drive them to their checkbooks to buy it. Dupe Data? I'll pass.

Now, I don't think a product's success is necessarily linked to its name. There's nothing compelling about Smucker's or Heinz or Dell. But I do know that people have to fall in love with a product to buy it, and the name can help to ignite the romance and spread the flame. Thus the power of the great names—Google, Amazon, iPod—in creating buzz around the capture phase of C + A + M = PG and fueling the initial success. There's just something intriguing and pleasing about these exceptional names.

And in the case of tech products, the name has another challenge: It has to dispel the notion that the product is complex, hard to use, and laden with manuals and help desks and nerd jargon and oh-God-why-did-I-buy-this-thing complexity. People want to know there is smart technology inside the box, but that using it is as easy as opening a box of Cracker Jack.

As we moved into think-tank mode, we asked ourselves, what does this software do in a simple way that the nontechnical person would understand—and how could we take a rather dry functionality and infuse it with instant cool? After hours of scribbling on a whiteboard a mélange of miserable names, near misses, and lame excuses for creativity, we said, "This thing is really like an e-boomerang. You take the data, toss it into storage, and when you need it, it flies right back into your desktop like a homing pigeon." However, given that the name Boomerang was tied up with intellectual property rights, we voted for redBoomerang, and we had the kind of slam-bang name we were searching for. We knew as soon as we said the word "Boomerang" that the analogy was descriptive, compelling, and memorable. And it removed the fear of technology from a technology product and made it fun by creating a metaphor for what it does and how easy it is to use.

With the name all set, we felt the pressure of the axiom "Nothing happens until a sale is made" hovering over us: We needed to make sales, to attract customers, to generate revenue, to build a user base, and to create a head of stream.

To make certain we gained attention in a marketplace saturated with marketing messages, we went beyond the use of words alone, deploying actual red boomerangs imprinted with the Web domain www.redboomerang.com.

The red boomerangs we sent to targeted prospects landed on the right desks, created instant appeal, and opened the doors to initial buyers. Initially, we were seeking to capture influencers who would drive large-quantity purchases, such as chief technology officers at colleges and universities, who would provide redBoomerang to their student base. Sending the actual boomerang served as a teaser. For example, a senior manager at Rutgers University became one of the product's first adopters after he received the boomerang.

Given that e-mail and snail-mail boxes are crammed with postcards, flyers, brochures, and catalogs, we recognized that a boomerang with nothing more than a domain address would pique the interest of our prospects and open the door in this critical phase of the capture process.

We wanted air cover, too. While the boomerangs were in the hands of our core market, we wanted them to be exposed to the product through media stories that would reinforce its unique and valuable capabilities.

Media pitches for the product reflected the nonthreatening whimsical approach to capturing first users.

Rampaging Hippopotamus Tears Through Researchers' Campsite and Tramples All Equipment

That was the case yesterday morning on the plains of the Serengeti, when an out of control hippopotamus charged through Silver Line's research campsite. Silver Line, Inc. was set up on location, performing tests and research on a new possible drug found in one of the local plants. The hippo made a mad dash for a head of lettuce, which was not properly stored in the food locker. En route to the safari salad, the hippo trampled over thousands of dollars' worth of computer equipment, causing Silver Line to lose their precious documents.

Fortunately, the aggressive hippopotamus hurt no one. Jack Pillar was the closest witness.

"It was amazing. She just came running through, nothing or no one could stop her. She pummeled hundreds of pounds' worth of equipment. That really goes to

show you the strength of these animals. I mean, it's going to cost money to replace this stuff, but hey, you can't stop Mother Nature."

When asked about his company's lost files, he stated: "We are not extremely worried about them. You see, we didn't lose them completely. We use redBoomerang to back up all of our files. So in a situation such as this one, we can get them back instantly."

After the hungry hippo snagged her lettuce, she moved on, and hasn't been seen since. And who said you can't get a free lunch?

Silver Line has made arrangements to replace the damaged equipment so the research can continue. The company's workers claim from now on they are going to be extra careful with snacks lying around the campsite. Pillar also stated he was particularly glad the animal was an herbivore.

The media pitch ended by driving the reader from the conceptual picture to a detailed description of the product to be found at www.redboomerang.com. This created a firm handshake between the cool tease of the branding and a pragmatic demonstration of the product's value proposition.

Amplify

Amplification is the process of enriching and expanding customer relationships. This doesn't happen by accident. It occurs only when companies—whether large or small—recognize that they must consistently raise the bar on what they do and how they do it. Minus this quest for ever-greater quality, variety, novelty, and innovation, your business unit is vulnerable to customer fatigue. The *love* that brought them to you in the first place will fade, and they will go elsewhere.

Think of how often you have "lost that lovin' feeling," too. The hotel, restaurant, clothing store, or fitness center that you once adored—and that took your patronage for granted by failing to grow the relationship with you—is now your former favorite hotel, restaurant, clothing store, or fitness center. Conversely, managers who focus on amplifying customer relationships drive loyalty to their business units and increase revenue per customer relationship through the cultivation of longevity, cross-selling, and increasing gross sales.

Amplifying customer relationships drives home a key principle of the C + A + M = PG equation: Successful managers understand that their business must be based not only on transactions, but also, more important, on a customer continuum. As you manage your business unit, eschew the notion that the goal is to capture a customer, celebrate, and move on. Next!

Surprisingly (because it is so limiting and self-defeating), this is the common practice.

But the celebration can never end. Because it is the relationship you must celebrate, not simply the capture.

Fairmont Hotels are superb at amplifying customer relationships. For years, I rejected Fairmont in favor of what I perceived to be superior choices: Ritz-Carlton and Four Seasons. That changed when a client booked me at the Fairmont Waterfront in Vancouver, British Columbia, Canada. From the moment I walked through the doors on a cold and dreary December evening, I felt special warmth based on extraordinary attention to detail. The people at Fairmont create an exceptional customer experience by exceeding my expectations at every turn.

I remember the bright-faced young woman at the check-in desk when I arrived the first night.

DESK HOST: You look as if you've had a long day, Mr. Stevens. I've upgraded you to a harbor-view suite so when you awake in the morning you'll enjoy a lovely panorama.

MS: That sounds delightful. Thank you.

DESK HOST: It's more than a pleasure, Mr. Stevens. May I send a complimentary cup of tea to your room now? It has a wonderful way of chasing away the evening chills.

That first night was more than a stay at a hotel. It was the start of a love affair I am still having with Fairmont for two years and counting. I still believe that the Ritz and the Four Seasons are more luxurious and more finely appointed. But Fairmont has pursued my heart and mind, and I have succumbed.

Fairmont is a lesson in the art and science of amplifying customer relationships. How they turned what would otherwise have been a one-night stand into a romance was based on a carefully constructed strategy designed to build on each successful visit and achieve a crescendo effect that seals the customer in a cocoon of pleasure, excitement, discovery, luxury, and intimacy.

The key to amplifying customer relationships is a nonstop focus on enhancing the customer's experience with your business unit:

Once I was a devotee of the Fairmont Waterfront (and I demonstrated that through repeat visits), I was exposed through mailings to my home and e-mails to the office to other Fairmont properties in popular business centers. There were smashing e-mails featuring exotic beachfront properties and artfully constructed brochures painting fabulous tableaux of charming ski holidays. I wanted to do it all!

As I began to radiate out along the Fairmont map, I was introduced to additional Fairmont resort properties. My wife and I spent a glorious weekend at New York's Plaza Hotel and a late spring fortnight at the Fairmont Princess in Bermuda. With the Stevens-Fairmont relationship growing, I was invited to join the Fairmont President's Club. This brought a rich lode of privileges and offers, from VIP check-in to complimentary upgrades. The more intense the romance became (as evidenced by my growing number of Fairmont visits around the world), my ranking in the President's Club was raised automatically, delivering an ever-greater bounty of rewards without my ever having to ask for it. This culminated in a free vacation at a Fairmont resort.

A wonderful expression of gratitude, to be sure, but in the truest form of amplification, just icing on the cake. Fairmont management orchestrated that critical transformation from a one-night stand to a romance through extraordinary service. Service to perfection. To a *T*. Delivered by every member of the hotel staff, from the concierge to the chambermaids.

And then to the pièce de résistance.

Checking out at the Waterfront roughly a year after my first visit, a colleague who had been traveling with me had a conversation with the front-desk manager.

COLLEAGUE: How is it that everyone in this hotel appears to know Mr. Stevens?

DESK MANAGER: Whenever a platinum-level President's Club member is visiting us, we circulate his photo to the staff prior to his arrival.

COLLEAGUE: Where do you get the photo?

DESK MANAGER: We do a Google search and take it from the
Web. If that fails, we ask the person's assistant
to send us one.

A perfect example of how great managers quietly and invisibly deliver exceptional results. And the Fairmont example reveals how exceptional management makes its way from the executive office (where it is generated) to the marketplace (where is it consumed and appreciated).

Maintain

Maintain means doing everything possible to keep customers loyal for life. This involves all of the tools and initiatives included in the "Capture" and "Amplify" section plus a program that retrieves lapsed customers and an action plan that seeks to "block the door" through positive reinforcement of the customer experience. As managers tackle this objective, the knee-jerk response is to turn to a standard-issue, points-based loyalty program. But not so fast. Customer loyalty is less about points and more about state of mind. It is reflected in personal conviction: *I want to consume the products and/or services associated with this brand.*

Rewards support the loyalty decision. The state of mind. They are not the drivers. They are the icing on the cake.

As you engage in the maintain component of the

C + A + M = PG equation, recognize that the most effective loyalty initiatives begin with an assessment of the company's value proposition/brand promise and customer base and radiate out from there. Companies that are superb at maintaining their customers (think Hertz, Starbucks, Harrah's) engage in this organic process of building on the values that drive the customer to the business in the first place. Sure, Hertz customers can win points every time they rent a Hertz car, but they return over and over again because they know they can count on Hertz for fast service, clean cars, on-board navigation systems, and frequent airport shuttles—all the little things that loom large when it comes to managing the headache known as business travel.

Companies that excel at the maintain component of C + A + M romance their customers. They know there is a difference between *loyalty* and *captivity (trying to keep you glued to the business for the fear of forfeiting points),* and what often poses as loyalty programs are actually captivity programs in disguise. So they eschew captivity in favor of loyalty, which is driven by embracing customers as opposed to holding them hostage to rewards.

Interestingly, the experts at maintaining customers are not the men and women with loyalty-program director in their titles. That distinction belongs to the managers who have launched and/or grown business units with the recognition that this could only be accomplished if customers remained loyal to the business and, in turn, drove their growth through consistent and expanded patronage.

Was Sam Walton a loyalty expert? The insular world of loyalty experts would say no, but Walton's customers are living embodiments of loyalty. Was Walt Disney a loyalty expert? Again, the gurus would say no, but generation after generation of families are Disney customers. The same for Michael Dell and Ray Kroc and Starbucks chairman Howard Schultz—as well as countless other lesser-known figures whose loyalty prowess springs from their business acumen. The fact is that exceptional loyalty is generated by businesspeople who understand that the foundation for this customer commitment must be a superior product or service or fusion of both. Once the winning business model is established and executed, the loyalty machinery (points/discounts/offers/rewards) can be applied to the foundation.

As you focus on romancing your customers to maintain them for life, ask yourself these key questions:

- Who are we as a business?
- What do we offer customers that is exceptional?
- What is our brand promise?
- How can we deliver this with near-flawless execution?
- How can we evolve so that we continue to thrill our customers?

IN COMPANY AFTER COMPANY, customers who stop buying are treated as so many names deleted from the database. But wait, these aren't names on a database. They are men and women, children and adults, singles and families, gays and straights, seniors and boomers, small spenders and big, who—for some reason—have *failed to remain loyal to the business.*

That's the traditional/comfortable/don't-blame-us view. Actually, *the business failed to remain loyal to their customers.* Failed to reward, excite, intrigue, fulfill, and make them feel special.

Precisely where failure occurs is often unknown since customer loss is simply viewed as a fact of life, the inevitable ebb and flow of business relationships. Managers tell themselves reassuring but deceptive lies:

- People simply want to try new experiences.
- Customers can't resist a competitor's lower prices.
- People are fickle; they are never loyal to any business.

Nonsense. The fact is:

- Most managers don't really know why they lose customers.
- Shame on them, they don't try to find out and to win them back.

Recently, after a hike at a wilderness reservation near my home, I drove to the deli that's been a favorite pit stop of mine after hours of wandering through the forest. Because I had to gas up my SUV first, I approached the shop from a side street off my usual route and noticed for the first time an almost identical and equally nondescript deli a block away. The only difference between the two was that my new discovery had promotional signs posted on the windows:

$$Soup * Salad * Beverage = \$6.00$$
$$Eggs * Bagel * Coffee = \$3.50$$

The prices were much lower than at the shop I'd been loyal to for years, but not enough to make me want to change venues. Not yet.

But, that very day, for the first time in years of eating there, I asked Sebastian, the owner of *my* deli, if I could use the men's room.

"No! It's for employees only."

OK, consider how I viewed this "no" from a customer's (fuming!) perspective. The owner of the shop:

- Declined to allow a rock-solid customer to use the restroom
- Didn't bother to explain why or to say, "Sorry"
- Had no idea of my name, though he'd served me hundreds of times

And that's when *my* deli's higher prices, which I would have been willing to continue to pay, became an issue that hit me for the first time—not because the split-pea soup, turkey sandwich, and diet Coke I ordered that day cost $11.30, and not because I was paying nearly double the competition's price. But because I was being treated with disdain for the *privilege* of doing so! They had me as a customer. They had captured me. Amplify the relationship? Maintain it? *Screw that!*

You can likely guess the next chapter of this story:

- I switched to the competitive deli.
- The prices were as advertised, and the food just as good.
- A spotless restroom was always available.

On my first visit, the friendly woman behind the counter asked my name, then added "Is that your beautiful golden retriever out there in the car?"

"Yes, that's my dog, Blue."

And then she entered sainthood.

"He is so cute."

This tale of two delis is centered on small businesses, but it's hardly a small story. The same scenario plays out daily at the likes of Kmart, Gateway, and Seattle's Best Coffee, as some of their customers switch to Wal-Mart, Dell, and Starbucks. They are said to have abandoned their providers. But did I abandon my favorite deli or did it abandon me?

Clearly, the latter. But most managers don't want to admit they abandon their customers. Because they don't live by the *universal equation* and the overwhelming power of C + A + M = PG, it is so much easier to write off customer losses to "the forces of nature" and ignore this as inevitable.

The problem (actually, the *opportunity* for you) is that most managers have blind spots. They view the customer as a number, don't recognize when that customer is gone, and fail to do anything to win him back once he's gotten away.

About a year ago, my wife and I purchased home accessories from a catalog company by the name of Ballard Designs. When the merchandise arrived (our first and only Ballard purchase), we were disappointed by the overall quality as well as the condition of one of the items delivered to us. We called customer service, the issue was politely handled, the merchandise was returned, and the proper credit was applied to our credit card.

That's exactly the way the textbooks say you should do it in the business unit you now manage or will manage in the future. But it totally misses the point. Ballard was fine at managing the return process but miserable at keeping a customer it had worked so hard and paid so much (through promotional mailings) to capture. We came into its world and left almost immediately, yet no one seemed to have the heart, the energy, the drive, and the determination to keep us as customers. Easy come, easy go. Actually, it was worse than that, because there was nothing easy (or inexpensive) about capturing us.

To cut to the chase, my wife and I have never purchased any-thing from Ballard again, yet, in a wasteful exercise (from the perspective of hard costs and opportunity costs), the com-pany continues to engage in a dumb and illogical autopilot program that fails to invite my wife and me back as customers (I don't think they know we left), ask why we abandoned them (or face the hard fact that *they abandoned us*), and offer us an inducement to try them again. Instead, the company continues to send forests of catalogs to our house (they must love to toss thousand-dollar bills out the window).

If you are thinking this is an anomaly, just the opposite is true. It is how most business is conducted. Storage USA (SUSA), a self-storage company that was part of GE but was sold by GE in 2005, served hundreds of thousands of cus-tomers a year. In one sense, it was a wonderful business (you build the storage centers and customers will come), but it was marred by the fact that these customer relationships tend to be short-lived. Not only because the ser-vice sucks, but also because the immediate need that drives the customers to seek self-storage is fleeting. Or so the company thought, be-cause it failed to consider the power of C + A + M . . . and failed to live by it.

Let's peer behind the curtain.

● The market for self-storage is driven by people who move, get divorced, or whose loved one dies, and whose furniture needs to be warehoused until it is relocated, redistributed, or sold.

● Typically, the tenant stays for three months. Most of the players in the self-storage industry give away the first month free as a promotional inducement.

● Therefore, thousands of self-storage centers (the industry is overbuilt) compete for two-month paid tenants. Three months after they move in on a first-month-free lease, they are on their way out. As soon as you get me, you lose me.

To many, this is the built-in negative of the business. But is it?

The tenant's apparent short-term need is not the real problem. No, the real problem is management's refusal at many self-storage companies to challenge and address the underlying causes of the move-in/move-out market dynamic. Just because the business has been driven for years by the natural market forces (divorce, relocation, death) that drive short-terms rentals doesn't mean warrior managers should accept this as the industry's primary driver of the business. Self-storage can have a wide range of long-term uses for millions who want to keep collectibles safe, make more room in their homes, reclaim their garages and closets, and store business supplies.

But the industry never opened its eyes to the possibilities

of storage. Never took steps to turn the two-month here-today-gone-tomorrow tenant into a long-term customer. Never challenged the idea that self-storage has to be a three-month blink-and-they're-out-of-here business.

That's why SUSA management (this was several years ago when GE still owned the business) decided it was time to declare constructive war on the industry. Step by step, SUSA (prompted in part by MSCO) looked beyond natural market forces to give more people reason to lease self-storage space for years and even decades.

We moved to the maintain component of C + A + M, acting to plug the holes in the leaking boat. Immediately, we began to look at every customer's move-in day as more than a ho-hum rite of passage that would lead to a quick and inevitable exit. No, we would do everything possible to block the exit doors with service and offers and value and customer commitment.

We would begin by viewing the storage business differently.

- *Traditional view.* A move-in is scheduled. Make sure the storage unit is clean and available and that an attendant is on-site to monitor the process.

- *Declare war view.* We have a new customer. We intend to maintain him. To provide more than space. To build a relationship. One that endures and grows through the leasing of additional space and referrals to friends and business associates.

The SUSA maintain strategy was executed through an integrated marketing plan that employed the key components of identifying creative uses for self-storage, developing killer offers, and building customer relationships.

- *Creative uses.* SUSA's public-relations strategy began to drive the recognition that self-storage can serve as the "Safe Deposit for Everything You Treasure." In seeking to change the public's perception, we promoted alternative ways to store one's treasures and business assets, keeping homes and offices well organized and clutter-free.

- *Killer offers.* Garden-variety "sales" don't cut it anymore. Ten percent off? Prices *slashed* by 20 percent? No one sees this as irresistible. Why? Because it's just so much noise. Every company says the same things. And consumers know the catches in the fine print:

UP TO 25 PERCENT OFF*†

*On special merchandise only
†Not valid during holiday periods

Killer offers blow all of that away. They are meant to be irresistible deals. For our storage client, we developed an offer no storage user could ignore: **six months free**. Six months free? Isn't that just giving the product away? No!

SUSA called it the abandonment offer: "Bring in a competitor's lease, break it for us, and we'll give you six months free rent on a one-year lease."

Because SUSA limited the offer to problem properties where the storage space would go empty without a killer offer, the impact on revenue management would be positive. The company wasn't cannibalizing inventory; it was maximizing its revenue potential.

Relationship Building

Building effective relationships means that you don't stand by and watch a customer vanish from your database and then view this loss as a statistical issue. When a company bases its growth on the C + A + M equation, it recognizes that it has to fight to capture its customers and fight just as hard to grow and keep its hard-won relationships with them. And it recognizes the stupidity of spending a fortune on marketing designed to woo customers through the door, only to let them walk down the exit ramp without any attempt to keep them in the fold. To sustain the romance. To stoke the relationship. Would you do that with a person you truly loved? Of course not! Why? Because it would hurt like hell. You should start thinking of customers as lovers. Feel the romance. Anticipate the pain. Bar the door!

Why are managers at leading companies (as well as their counterparts at small, entrepreneurial-owned and -managed businesses) willing to let customers walk away? Scot-free. Without a fight. Minus a real or metaphorical bouquet of flowers to win them back. Zero. *Nada.* Not even a phone call that goes like this:

• Why did you leave? Did we do something to insult or disappoint you?

• We miss you, we treasure you, and we want to keep you as a customer.

• To demonstrate our commitment to you, we are sending you a box of chocolates as a token of our sweet thoughts.

• Is there anything else we can do to have the pleasure of serving you again? Anything?

In 99 percent of companies, this mating dance never occurs, because customers are treated as statistics, and no one is going to romance a spreadsheet. And therein lies the problem, and the opportunity. Even those people in a business trained in customer-relationship management and loyalty programs focus on metrics. In fact, they are often the worst culprits. While they are digitizing the issue, you—the warrior manager—can personalize it.

To put this in perspective, imagine that a good acquaintance (one you hear from five or six times a year) suddenly goes AWOL. Drops off the radar screen and is nowhere to be found. Would you:

- Try to call the missing person to discover what happened and why?

- Send an e-mail?

- Ask a friend about the "missing" party?

You would do all of the above. Of course you would. But why don't business managers do the same (or something close to it) when customers disappear? When they stop buying and flee to the competition?

My experience tells me it's because these managers:

- Don't care about the loss of a couple of customers, a couple of hundred, or a couple of thousand. (To their dangerous way of thinking, *there are plenty of fish in the sea.*)

- Don't know the customers have left.

- Believe that the wholesale loss of customers is inevitable.

- Are not about to beg customers to come back.

- Are *too busy* to do anything about the loss of their most valuable assets.

Each and every one of these reasons demonstrates with the subtlety of an air-raid siren that most managers actually live by the following guideline (although they don't know it or won't admit it):

CAPTURE AND LET WHATEVER THE HELL HAPPENS AFTER THAT HAPPEN.

If you're thinking that the intensity with which a company seeks to maintain each and every customer or client should somehow reflect the size of the business, you are not only wrong, you are inadvertently planning the company's demise. Revlon's founder Charles Revson used to take turns at the company's customer-service switchboard, asking women what they liked or disliked about Revlon products. Every single complaint was treated as if it was voiced by a million dissatisfied women staging a protest rally at the beauty empire's New York headquarters. Revson knew that there are ways to monitor customer satisfaction and loyalty no matter how many names are on the database. Equally important, he also knew that once a manager takes comfort in the fact that the business is not dependent on any single customer, it slides down the Olympic downhill of arrogance, sloppiness, and complacency. Wow, do hungry competitors love that.

The Journey Within

Some years ago I interviewed nearly fifty men and women, all graduates of Harvard's famed Advanced Management Program—a twelve-week intellectual boot camp for senior executives. All were experienced managers with many years at the controls of corporate business units or entrepreneurial companies. All had developed precise and carefully honed methods of managing, as well as elaborate belief systems that validated their methodologies as "the only way to do it right."

And virtually all experienced a dramatic transformation upon reentry from the boot camp to their once-familiar routines in the business world. At some point during the Harvard course, it struck them that they had become prisoners of their once-vaunted managerial routines and, for this reason, were no longer truly the masters of their destinies. In fact, they were slaves to habit, order, and blind obedience to what "is" as opposed to what "can be."

Seeing their world through the prism of an exhilarating and enlightening experience opened a new universe of options. And they pounced. Some rethought their marriages and divorced. Others came face-to-face with the realization that their management style was the greatest impediment to the success of their business units. Still others discarded their patient timetables for promotion to higher positions and pursued accelerated paths to the next levels of managerial rank and responsibility.

All were cautious and conservative members of the corporate elite. Not a wild-eyed dreamer in the group. But each and every one abandoned tightly guarded and highly rationalized beliefs and made fundamental changes in their practices.

Their heads turned 180 degrees. Something powerful reshaped their lives. Your turn!

Start by freeze-framing what you have learned in reading this book. In taking this crash course.

Every time I give a speech, I advise my audience,

Don't go back to the office.

I know they do have to return to work. To the hodgepodge of issues big and small that are frantic to reclaim their brains. But before they dive into this business-as-usual scenario, I want them to isolate at least one insight they have gained and to contemplate how they will apply it to their management process.

I offer the same advice to you. Having completed this book, your mind is likely filled with new information, fresh perspectives, original ideas, and intriguing thoughts about changing many of the practices you once viewed as near-sacred components of sound management. The question is, how should you process and implement all of this? Again I advise, "Don't go back to the office." Not until you complete the following exercise.

- Jot down the three most important, compelling, or intriguing issues that surfaced during your reading of this book.
- Think about how you can incorporate them into your managerial agenda, adopting new practices and/or discarding others.
- Give yourself a deadline for acting on at least one of the Big Three (no later than two weeks from now) and create a timeline for acting on all three within two months.

Most important, recognize that you are engaging in a process that may be entirely new to you: declaring war on yourself. And on your business unit. Constructive war, yes, but war is war. And that may be a hard concept to accept as you move beyond the crash course to the obstacle course that you face in building an ever-more-successful career.

As you challenge *conventional wisdom,* be aware that it is a stubborn adversary. You will have to hold it up to the light, see it for what it is, and—empowered with the knowledge you have gained—have the conviction and the guts to reverse key pillars of your belief system.

Think of this post-course period as a journey of discovery. One that is focused within you. All of your life you have turned outside for knowledge—to schools and mentors and Web searches and classrooms. Look at your calendar—chances are good that there are seminars and conventions and corporate-training programs filling up your dance card. But the period of learning you have now entered is different: It is a time for introspection, absorption, and deciphering the best course of action to identify and unleash the latent power and potential in the evolving you.

Take the time to engage in this discovery. I assure you that you will marvel at the wonders you will uncover. All too often people march through life like Soviet soldiers goose-stepping to a military march. They are headed where they have been pointed by parents and teachers and the myriad of influencers who impact their lives.

Yes, we all need advice and counsel from those we respect. But the wisest and most successful among us stop the music now and then, take stock (witness Bill Gates during his Think Weeks), and decide what they want to change, refine, augment, or completely reengineer before stepping on the accelerator again. Notice how the goose-steppers all around you never explore the options at their disposal. The different paths they can take. They just keep marching. They may arrive at their destination expeditiously, but where are they going? How blind they are! How visionary you can and should be!

 he future is yours. Seize it.

Notes

1. Interview, June 17, 1994, Las Vegas, Nevada. Academy of
   Achievement, www.achievement.org.

2. Interview, February 12, 1991, New York, New York. Academy of
   Achievement, www.achievement.org.

3. Ibid.

4. Alice Calaprice, ed. *The Quotable Einstein.* Princeton, N.J.:
   Princeton University Press, 1996.

5. Interview, May 23, 1998, Jackson Hole, Wyoming. Academy of
   Achievement, www.achievement.org.

6. Interview, June 19, 1991, Washington, D.C. Academy of
   Achievement, www.achievement.org.

7. Interview, May 16, 1991, San Diego, California. Academy of
   Achievement, www.achievement.org.

Index

F

facts, questioning of, 196
failure to act, 29
Fairmont Hotels, 268–71
family-owned businesses,
    61–62, 149–53
Father Knows Best (TV sit-
    com), 140–41
fear, 29, 54, 125–36
    confrontation of, 125
    declaring war on, 133–36
    of firing employees, 130–33
    forms of, 125–29
    reaction based on, 133–34
FedEx, 184–85
Feynman, Richard, 108
Fiorina, Carly, 106
firing employees, 130–33
first-strike philosophy, 190–91
Ford, Henry, 79, 100, 180
Four Seasons, 88, 268, 269
Franklin, Benjamin, 13–14
Friedland, Dion, 19–20

G

Gates, Bill
    commitment to self-
        improvement of, 17–18
    credibility of, 214
    leadership and, 106, 108, 109
    taking stock by, 291

Gateway, 276
GE (General Electric), 28,
    280
General Motors (GM), 48, 79
Gerstner, Lou, 200–202
going out of business, 28–29
going-out-of-business-slowly
    scenario, 29, 82–83
Goldberg, Ken, 260–62
Goldman Sachs, 176
gold-standard companies,
    85–90
Google, 31, 214, 263
grand unifying theory (GUT),
    254
growing a business, 30, 80–81
    blocking and tackling and,
        81–85
    breakthrough opportunities
        and, 81, 83, 84, 85
    C+A+M equation and,
        254–85
    corporate life cycles and,
        27
    obstacles to, 21–22
    strategies for, 21–22, 25–26,
        84–85

H

Harrah's, 272
Hartford Life Insurance, 241
Harvard Business School, 27

L

Land, Edwin, 15
Lauder, Estée, 79
leaders, 104–57
    caretakers vs., 61–62
    continuous learning by,
        18–19
    in family-owned businesses,
        61–62, 149–53
    fear of managing and,
        125–36
    imagination as quality of, 188
    management blueprint and,
        153, 156, 258
    need for approval and,
        111–16
    skill development by,
        105–11
    strength/weakness assess-
        ment of, 109–11
learning, importance of, 16,
    18–20, 54, 219
Lehman Brothers, 153–54
Levitt, Bill, 62–64
Levittown, New York, 64
life-insurance industry, 47, 78,
    124–25, 241–42
lodging/hospitality industry,
    88–90, 268–71
love of product or service,
    30–31
loyalty, customer, 271–77
Lucas, George, 185–86

M

MacArthur, Douglas, 148
Machiavelli, Niccolò, 189
magazine publishing industry,
    202–6
maintaining customers,
    271–82
management persona, 46, 51,
    107
managerial philosophy, 28,
    38–64
    absence of, 48
    identification of, 60–64
    manager weaknesses and,
        45–48
    for MSCO Inc., 51–55
    need for, 48–49, 55–60
managers
    caretakers vs. leaders as,
        61–62
    characteristics of successful,
        16–17
    credibility of, 214
    dispensability of, 130–31,
        243
    80/20 rule and, 250–51
    fear and, 54, 125–36
    firing of employees by,
        130–33
    Killer Apps and, 170–96
    leadership by, 104–58
    micromanagement by, 67,
        68, 221

About the Author

MARK STEVENS, CEO of MSCO (www.msco.com), is one of the nation's leading experts in ROI-based marketing and the creator of the Extreme Marketing and Declare War on Your Business processes. Stevens is an entrepreneur, adviser, and business builder, and is the author of such prominent books as *Your Marketing Sucks, The Big Eight, Sudden Death: The Rise and Fall of F. F. Hutton, Extreme Management,* and *King Icahn: The Biography of a Renegade Capitalist.*